Over 100 Delicious Deep Fryer Recipes

How To Use Your Deep Fryer To Prepare An Endless
Number Of Mouth Watering Fried Foods For
The Whole Family!

Author: A G Brown

You can achieve anything you desire if you will only believe.

Table of Content

Introduction

Most people around the world have a passion for deep fried foods that will never go away anytime soon. From mouth-watering fried chicken to fried ice cream and so much more, it's tough to beat the delicious taste of deep fried foods!

The key to success with cooking fried food is not just the recipe though. It also has a lot to do with being prepared, using the right type of oil and temperatures, as well as preparation.

This book will guide you in helping you cook up some of the best tasting fried foods you've ever had. You will find scrumptious recipes from all over the world so that you can try new foods and better enjoy old favorites. So let's get started because I'm getting hungry!

Deep Frying Basics

Oil

One of the things that many people don't realize is that not all cooking oils are alike. Different types of oils heat at different temperatures and produce various flavors in your foods.

Vegetable and canola oils are what most people use, but are they your best choice? While these oils will work fine for most, the best choice for oil in your home deep fryer is peanut oil.

Peanut oil has a very high smoking point and it lasts much longer than other oils in your fryer.

Commercial deep fryers in restaurants and other professional kitchens use high oleic canola oil. The main reason for this is due to the oil not breaking down as quickly with high temperatures and repeated uses. Cooks will often strain and reuse the same oil multiple times.

For home deep fryers, peanut oil is your number one choice.

Temperatures

The biggest key to deep frying success is by selecting the right temperature to cook your foods in. Too low of a heat setting and the cooking oil soaks into your foods…too high and you get foods that cook too quickly on the outside and not cooked thoroughly on the inside.

All cooking oils have a "smoking point", which is simply the point at which the oil begins to smoke before bursting into flames. Some oils, like an extra virgin olive oil, can begin smoking at 330 degrees F, while peanut oil can go as high as 470 degrees F before smoking.

The best tip here is to follow the manufacturer's guidelines for temperatures settings on your particular fryer. Generally speaking you will want to cook most foods at 350 – 390 degrees F.

If for some reason your deep fryer does not have a thermostat, you can drop a small piece of food into the heated oil and look for a full rolling boil to form around it. If it does, the oil is then ready for use.

Replacing Your Oil

How can you know when it is time to change out your cooking oil? Any cooking oil will break down after normal use. The high heat, water and food particles that are left behind all contribute to the oil breaking down.

Look for these indicators to determine when you should change the oil:

- Foods become discolored and much darker than normal
- Oil smokes at normal cooking temperatures
- You notice odors coming up from the oil
- Foaming around the foods cooking in the oil

Some will say you can filter the old oil or strain it to get more use out of it, but I do not recommend it. For home deep fryers, dispose of the old oil and pour in a new batch. You'll have much better tasting food.

I would also not recommend you storing oil in the refrigerator. It attracts moisture and breaks down faster, as well as creating a problem with spattering as the cold oil heats up to hot.

Safety Tips

Never overfill your deep fryer with oil. There should be a "fill line" in your fryer to use as a guide in refilling it.

Never heat your oil at higher temperatures than the recommended manufacturer's settings.

Do not put water in hot oil. Spattering will occur and injury to your eyes or face can easily happen.

Do not use your fingers to lower or pick up foods. Use a pair of kitchen tongs or a strainer to lower or remove your food.

Always follow your manufacturer's guidelines for your deep fryer and you should not have any cooking issues.

1
Deep Fryer Italian Zeppole

Ingredients:
>2-1/2 cups all purpose flour
>1/8 tsp. salt
>2-1/2 cups water
>1/2 cup white wine
>Olive oil
>1 Tbs. ground cinnamon
>1 cup sugar

Sift flour and salt together in a bowl and set aside. Combine water and wine in a saucepan over medium high heat. Do not boil. When bubbles appear on the bottom of the pan, add flour mixture all at once. Stir constantly with a wooden spoon until dough comes together into a ball.

Transfer to a lightly oiled work surface. Pound with a rolling pin about 10 minutes until smooth. Roll dough into strips about 1/2 inch around. Cut into 8 inch lengths and pinch ends together to make rings.

Heat oil in deep fryer to 375F. Without overcrowding, deep fry 2-3 pieces at a time 3-4 minutes until golden, pricking each one with a skewer as it fries. Drain on absorbent paper. Combine cinnamon and sugar in a bowl. Dip zeppole in sugar mixture while still hot.

2
Deep Fryer Sopaipillas

Ingredients:
>1 cup all purpose flour
>1/2 tsp. salt
>1/2 tsp. baking powder
>1-1/2 tsp. nonfat dry milk
>1 tsp. vegetable shortening
>1/2 cup cold water

Heat oil in deep fryer to 370F – 380F. Combine flour and next 4 ingredients in a food processor and pulse 3-4 times. With machine running, pour in water through feed tube and process about 15 seconds, or until ingredients begin to come together.

Transfer mixture to a lightly floured work surface and mix by hand, adding more flour as needed, to make soft dough. Roll into a circle about 1/8 inch thick and cut each circle into 12 wedges. Add 2 or 3 at a time to fry basket.

Lower into hot oil and fry 5-7 minutes, turning several times, until golden. Drain on absorbent paper and repeat with remaining sopaipillas. Serve with honey, syrup, guacamole or salsa

3
Spicy Hot Chicken Bits

Ingredients:
- 3 pounds boneless chicken breasts without skin
- 1/8 teaspoon salt
- 1/8 teaspoon garlic powder
- 2 tablespoons red pepper [or less]
- 1/2 teaspoon black pepper
- 1 cup flour

Wash chicken breasts and pat dry. Cut into 1-inch strips. Sprinkle chicken strips with salt and garlic powder, turning pieces so all sides are seasoned. Continue seasoning with red and black peppers.

Refrigerate for 1 hour to bring out the flavor of seasonings. Dust chicken with flour, then deep fry in oil at 370F, for 3 to 4 minutes. Drain on paper towels; serve with your favorite dipping sauce, or try one of the sauces below.

4
Cajun Fried Fish

Ingredients:
  2 pounds of fish fillets
  3 eggs, slightly beaten
  1/2 cup milk
  1/2 cup beer
  3 tablespoons prepared mustard
  1/2 to 1 teaspoon Tabasco sauce
  2 tablespoons salt, divided
  2 teaspoons black pepper, divided
  1/2 to 1 teaspoon cayenne pepper, divided, or to
  taste
  3 cups fine yellow corn flour

In a mixing bowl, whisk together eggs, milk, beer, mustard, Tabasco, and half of the salt and peppers. Cut fish fillets into bite sized pieces, or nuggets. Place fish in egg mixture, coating well; cover, refrigerate, and let soak for about 1 hour.

Mix corn flour with the remaining salt and peppers in a shallow, wide bowl or pie plate. Preheat oil in deep fryer to about 370F.

Remove fish from mixture and dredge with corn flour mixture. Fry fish until the fish nuggets float to the surface and turn golden brown, taking care not to overcook.

Place fish nuggets on paper towels to drain, patting gently with paper towels to blot up excess oil. Use this batter to fry shrimp, oysters, and other shellfish. Serves 4

5
Jalapeno Poppers

Ingredients:
> 12 jalapeno peppers, sliced in half lengthwise, seeds removed
> 8 ounces cream cheese, room temperature
> 2 eggs, beaten
> 2 tablespoons water
> Dash salt
> 1 cup plain dry breadcrumbs

Fill jalapeno pepper halves with cream cheese and press halves back together. Combine eggs, water and salt. Dip jalapeno peppers into egg mixture and into breadcrumbs. Place on a cookie sheet and freeze for 2 hours.

Heat oil in deep fryer to 370F. Deep fry peppers in batches for about 3 minutes, or until golden brown. Transfer jalapeno poppers to paper towels to drain.

6
Homemade Potato Chips

Ingredients:
> 6 or more medium to large potatoes
> Salt

Wash and peel the potatoes. Slice very thin. An old fashioned cabbage slicer can be used (careful of the fingers) or use a sharp knife or food processor with a thin slicing blade.

Put the slices at once into a bowl of cold water and let stand for at least one hour. Ice water is best, but you can set the whole bowl in the refrigerator if you wish. Dry well by shaking them in a towel.

Fry in hot oil at 390F. until a light golden brown. Don't try frying too many at once, better to put one layer on the frying basket. Drain on paper towels or any kind of plain crumpled absorbent paper.

If you haven't any paper, use a worn dish towel. Salt lightly. These can be kept for some time if they are sealed into plastic bags or containers after they have cooled.

7
Crispy Fried Frog Legs

Ingredients:
> 2 to 2 1/2 pounds small frog legs
> 1/3 cup lemon juice
> Crushed ice
> 1/3 cup milk
> 2 eggs, separated
> 2 teaspoons vegetable oil
> Salt and pepper
> Dash cayenne pepper, optional
> 2 cups all-purpose flour

Wash frog legs thoroughly. Place in a large bowl; sprinkle with lemon juice, and cover with crushed ice. Refrigerate 1 to 3 hours. In a small bowl, whisk together milk, egg yolks, and 2 teaspoons oil.

Beat egg whites until stiff; fold into milk and egg yolk mixture. Sprinkle frog legs with salt and pepper, and a little cayenne, if using; dip each in milk-egg mixture, then dredge in flour.

Heat oil in a deep-fryer or skillet to 375F. Fry frog legs until golden brown. Remove with a slotted spoon and transfer to paper towels to drain.

8
Deep-Fried Twinkies

Ingredients:
   6 Twinkies
   Popsicle sticks
   Flour for dusting
   1 cup milk
   2 tablespoons vinegar
   1 Tablespoon oil
   1 cup flour
   1 teaspoon baking powder
   1/2 teaspoon salt

1. Chill or freeze Twinkies for several hours or overnight.

2. Heat 4 cups oil in deep fryer to about 375F.

3. Mix together milk, vinegar and oil.

4. In another bowl, blend flour, baking powder and salt.

5. Whisk wet ingredients into dry and continue mixing until smooth. Refrigerate while oil heats.

6. Push stick into Twinkie lengthwise, leaving about 2 inches to use as a handle, dust with flour and dip into the batter. Rotate Twinkie until batter covers entire cake.

7. Place carefully in hot oil. The Twinkie will float, so hold it under with a utensil to ensure even browning. It should turn golden in 3 to 4 minutes. Depending on the size of your deep fryer, you might be able to fry only one at a time, two at the most.

8. Remove Twinkie to paper towel and let drain. Remove stick and allow Twinkie to sit for about 5 minutes before serving.

9
Deep-Fried Smelts

Fresh smelts should be stored refrigerated at 32F to 40F [0C to 4C], excess liquid drained, packed into airtight containers and eaten within 3 to 4 days or 1 to 2 days when fried.

Smelts should be frozen at 0F [-18C], into airtight food containers, immediately after buying; bought frozen, smelts should be eaten within 4 to 6 months for maximum freshness.

Ingredients:
> 1 pound [454 g] smelts
> 1 cup [250 ml] milk
> Flour
> Salt, to taste
> Parsley sprigs
> 2 lemons, quartered

Into a deep-fryer, heat oil to 375F [190C]. Wipe dry smelts; dip smelts into milk, then coat with flour.

Deep-fry smelts into hot oil for 5 to 7 minutes, until golden.

Drains smelts onto paper towels and salt them. Arrange smelts onto a serving plate. Serve, decorated with parsley sprigs and lemon segments

10
Deep Fried Mars Bars

Ingredients:
     1 Mars bar (UK) or Milky Way (US)
     1 cup plain flour
     1/2 cup corn flour
     Pinch of bicarbonate of soda (baking soda to Yanks)
     Milk or beer

Chill the chocolate bar by keeping it in the fridge, but do not freeze it.

Mix the flours and bicarbonate of soda (baking soda) together. Add milk (traditional) or beer (which gives a lighter result) until you get a batter with the consistency of thin cream.

Heat oil in deep fryer to 375F. Remove wrapper from chilled chocolate bar. Coat bars completely in batter. Carefully lower into hot oil and fry until golden brown.

Serve, with ice cream or French fries, if you're so inclined. (Of course, if you want to be sophisticated, you can cut the bar into bite-sized pieces before coating in batter.)

11
Deep Fried Chitterlings

Ingredients:
  2 pounds chitterlings
  1 egg, lightly beaten
  1 tablespoon water
  Fine cracker crumbs

Clean and Prepare chitterlings: Wash chitterlings 3 or 4 times and place in a large kettle with 4 or 5 cups of water with 1 or 2 chopped onions, 2 bay leaves, 2 teaspoons salt, 1/4 teaspoon pepper, 2 cloves minced garlic, and other seasonings as desired.

Simmer for 2 hours or until chitterlings are tender. Beat egg with 1 tablespoon water. Cut boiled chitterlings into pieces about the size of oysters.

Dip each piece into egg mixture then roll in crumbs. Fry in oil at about 370F until golden brown.

12
Deep Fried Cod

Ingredients:
>1 lb. frozen cod
>1 egg
>3/4 cup flour
>1/2 cup water
>1 tsp salt
>1 tbs sesame seed

Mix ingredients together in bowl and set aside. Cut cod fillets into serving sizes.

Dip pieces into batter (make sure pieces are dry so batter will stick). Deep fry in 375F oil for 10 to 15 minutes each side or until golden brown.

13
Deep-Fried Squid

Ingredients:
> 3 lb Squid, cleaned and cut into rings
> 3 cups of flour for coating
> Salt and pepper to taste

Clean the squid and cut it into rings. Dry the rings thoroughly with paper towels.

Add salt and pepper to flour and dip squid rings into mixture.

Heat oil to 350F in deep fryer. Drop basket laden with one layer of
Squid into the oil. If you don't have a basket for deep frying, use a large spoon or tongs to immerse squid in oil, and to remove. Fry until coating turns golden brown, about 3 or 4 minutes.

Remove squid and drain. Turn down heat to moderate until just before you are ready to cook the next batch; oil will overheat when the fryer is empty. Remove excess oil from squid with paper towels.

Serve rings hot with any of the dipping sauces described below or with lemon wedges. Cole slaw is a natural with deep fried squid.

14
Cajun Deep Fried Turkey

Ingredients:
> 10 lb Turkey; up to 15 lbs
> 6 tsp Salt
> 6 tsp Paprika
> 6 tsp White pepper
> 6 tsp Cayenne
> 6 tsp Accent; opt
> 16 oz Liquid crab oil concentrate

NOTE-Not recommended for indoor cooking.

Rinse turkey inside and out. Mix 1 part crab boil concentrate to 4 parts water. Combine dry ingredients with crab boil solution. Adjust seasoning to taste. Inject turkey (approximately 2" apart) with mixture using syringe (available from gourmet kitchen stores.) Cover turkey with foil and refrigerate over night.

Heat oil to 350F. CAUTION: Use an oil thermometer to monitor the oil. Put turkey in basket and CAREFULLY lower it into the pot. Cook 5 minutes per pound. Check in 1 hour using a meat thermometer.

NOTE-This is a great dish, but should only be attempted by someone who has experience with doing this. It is also expensive due to the large amount of oil needed.

15
Apple Fritters/Deep Fried

Ingredients:
   1 large egg; beaten
   1 cup milk
   1 cup Apples (unpeeled apple which is finely diced
   or grated)
   1/4 cup sugar
   1/4 tsp salt
   1 tsp grated orange peel
   3 tbs orange juice
   2 tsp vanilla extract
   2 cup flour
   1 tbs baking powder
   Confectioner's sugar

In mixing bowl, combine beaten egg, milk, apple, sugar, salt, orange peel, orange juice and vanilla. Sift together the flour and baking powder; fold into the apple mixture, stir just until all flour is moistened. Drop batter by rounded teaspoon into hot oil (350F).

Fry until deep golden brown, about 3-4 minutes, turning once. Drain fritters thoroughly on paper towels. Roll in sugar or sift the sugar over the tops. Yield: about 40 fritters.

16
Karnabeet Makly (deep-fried cauliflower)

Ingredients:
> 1 large cauliflower
> 1 tsp salt
> Taratoor Sauce

Cut away the thick stem at the base of the cauliflower and remove the green leaves. Break the florets off the center core and cut the core into 1" cubes. Wash the florets and cubes under cold running water.

In a 3 to 4 qt enameled or stainless steel saucepan, bring 1 qt of water and the salt to a boil over high heat. Drop in the cauliflower and cook briskly, uncovered, for 10 minutes, or until the pieces are tender but still somewhat resistant to the point of a small, sharp knife. Drain in a sieve or colander.

Heat 1 - 2 inches of oil in deep fryer to 375F. Pat the cauliflower completely dry with paper towels, and a dozen or so pieces at a time, fry them in the hot oil for about 15 minutes, or until golden brown on all sides. As they brown, remove them with a slotted spoon and drain them on paper towels. They may be served hot or at room temperature covered with taratoor.

17
Deep Fried Shrimp Balls

Ingredients:
    1 lb Shrimp, cleaned & deveined
    2 bacon strips
    4 water chestnuts
    -OR-
    1/2 med onion
    Salt
    Pepper
    1 egg, beaten
    2 tbs corn starch

1. Mince shrimp, bacon, onion or water chestnuts together until fine. Place mixture in bowl. Remove crusts from bread. Dice bread into very fine cubes. Place cubes in shrimp mixture. Add salt, pepper, egg and 2 tablespoons corn starch to mixture. Combine thoroughly.

2. Fill deep fryer halfway up with oil. Heat oil to 385F.

3. When oil is ready for deep frying, take 2 teaspoons, dip into shrimp mixture and form a 1" diameter ball. Drop ball into hot oil. Place about 8 balls into the hot oil. Allow each ball to deep fry 3 minutes. Turn balls so that each will fry to a golden brown color.

4. Remove balls to paper toweling to drain excess oil from them. Repeat procedure for deep frying rest of shrimp mixture until all of the mixture is used up. Place shrimp balls on a serving platter. Garnish with parsley or other raw vegetable.

18
Ronieri's Deep Fried Parsley

Ingredients:
> 1 bunch parsley
> 1/4 cup flour
> 2 eggs, beaten
> 3/4 cup unseasoned bread crumbs
> Lawrey's Seasoned Salt

Wash the parsley, break off the tough stems and make small bunches of parsley heads. While parsley is still wet, dip into flour, then eggs, then into the bread crumbs. Shake off excess.

Heat oil to 375F. Place prepared parsley in the oil and fry until golden brown, about 50 seconds. Drain well and season to taste.

19
Gaudet's Deep Fried Pickles

Ingredients:
- 1 cup sour cream
- 1/4 cup prepared blue cheese dressing
- 1 16-oz jar sliced dill pickles
- 1/4 cup mayonnaise
- 2 tbs Dijon-style mustard
- 3 cup seasoned bread crumbs

Mix sour cream, mayonnaise, blue cheese dressing and mustard together in a serving bowl. Set aside.

Dip pickles in bread crumbs and deep-fry in oil at 350F until golden. Serve with sauce for dipping.

20
Deep Fried Tofu

Ingredients:
>1 lb tofu cut in 1/2 inch cubes
>1/2 cup wheat germ
>3 tbs cornstarch
>Soy sauce or sweet and sour sauce

1. Roll the tofu cubes in the wheat germ mixed with cornstarch. Heat oil to 350F

2. Fry the cubes, a few at a time, in a basket in the hot oil. Drain on paper towels and keep warm while making the remainder.

3. Serve with soy sauce or sweet and sour sauce dip.

21
Deep-Fried Devils (You Zha Gui or You Tiao)

Ingredients:
> 2 tsp coarse salt
> 1 tsp alum
> 1 tsp Ammonium carbonate powder
> 1 tsp baking soda
> 1 tsp baking powder
> 1 1/4 cup water at room temperature
> 3 1/2 cup unbleached flour (approx.)

Put the salt, alum ammonium carbonate, and baking soda and powder in a large mixing bowl. Add the water and stir until all the powders are dissolved.

Add 3 cups of the flour and use your hands in a pressing an pushing motions to mix the dough. Add the remaining flour if the dough is too soft. It should be firm enough to handle. Transfer the dough to a floured surface and knead until smooth with no lumps. The kneading should take no longer than 2 or 3 minutes.

Divide the dough into two pieces, and with a little flour shape them into two oblong loaves, then coat with oil and wrap tightly in plastic. Let them sit at least 4 hours and up to 8 hours at room temperature.

Sprinkle a large cutting board with flour and put it near the stove. Stretch the loaves so that each measures 14 inches long and 3 inches wide. Lay them on the board at least 4 inches apart. Sprinkle some flour on top. With a rolling pin, roll loaf out to about 1/4 inch thick, 4 inches wide, and 16 inches long. Repeat with the other loaf. Cover with a damp towel & let rest 10 minutes.

Heat 3 inches of oil to 350 F. Have a tray lined with paper towels nearby. Cut 4 crosswise strips 2/3 inch wide from one of the loaves. Brush the top of 2 with water, and then lay the other 2 on top. Press a chopstick lengthwise on each pair of strips to make them stick
together. Stretch each double strip to 8 to 10 inch length.

Lower the pieces into the oil, immediately turning them gently with chopsticks,
without squeezing them, until all sides become lightly browned. This takes about 2 minutes. Drain on paper towels. Repeat the cutting and frying with the rest of the dough.

Wrapped in plastic, they keep well 1 week in the refrigerator and 1 month in the freezer. Reheat in a pre-heated 450 F oven for about 2 minutes, until crisp but not dry.

22
Deep Fried Dill Pickle Fondue Balls

Ingredients:
>2 eggs whites, slightly beaten
>1 cup grated Swiss cheese
>1/3 cup dill pickles, chopped
>Dash garlic salt
>1/2 cup dry bread crumbs

Combine egg whites, Swiss cheese, chopped pickles and garlic salt. Drop by teaspoonfuls into the bread crumbs; roll and coat well while forming small balls. Chill until ready to serve.

Fry in deep fryer at 375 F until golden brown, about 2-3 minutes. Drain well on paper towels. Makes about 2 dozen appetizers.

23
Poori (Deep Fried Puffy Bread)

Ingredients:
> 1 cup sifted whole-wheat flour (sift to take out some of the larger bran bits)
> 1 cup all-purpose flour
> 1/2 teaspoon salt
> 2 tablespoons vegetable oil
> 1/2 cup water

Put the 2 flours and salt in a bowl. Drizzle the 2 tablespoons oil over the top. Rub the oil in with your fingers so the mixture resembles coarse breadcrumbs. Slowly add the water to form a stiff ball of dough. Move the ball on to a clean work surface. Knead it for 10-12 minutes or until it is smooth. Form a ball. Rub about ¼ teaspoon oil on the ball and slip it into a plastic bag. Set it aside for 30 minutes.

Knead the dough again, and divide it into 12 equal balls. Keep 11 of them covered while you work with the twelfth. Flatten this ball and roll it out into a 5-5 1/2" round. If you have the space, roll out all the porris and keep them in a single layer, covered with plastic wrap.

In a deep fryer fill about 1/3 with oil to 390 F. Meanwhile, line a platter with paper towels. Lift up one poori and lay it carefully over the surface of the hot oil. It might sink to the bottom but it should rise in seconds and begin to sizzle. Using the back of a slotted spoon, push the poori gently into the oil with tiny, swift strokes. Within seconds, the poori will puff up. Turn it over and cook the second side for about 10 seconds. Remove it with a slotted spoon and put it on the platter.

Make all the pooris this way. The first layer on the platter may be covered with a layer of paper towels. More pooris can then be spread over the top. Serve the pooris hot (immediately).

24
Deep Fried Prawns With Batter (Jow Ha)

Ingredients:
    1 lb prawns
    1 tsp salt
    3/4 cup flour
    2 tsp baking powder
    1 cup cornstarch
    1 Egg
    1 tbs oil
    3/4 cup water

Shell and devein prawns, leaving the tails on. Devein and clean. Sprinkle with salt and mix well. Refrigerate for two hours. Mix flour, baking powder, cornstarch, eggs, oil and water to make a batter.

Heat deep fryer to 375 F. Holding the prawns by the tails, dip in batter, and then drop into hot oil. Fry until golden, turning once. Drain. Serve hot.

Use cocktail sauce, chili sauce or sweet and sour sauce for dipping. One cup prepared biscuit mix may be substituted for the flour and baking powder.

25
Sri Lanka Murukku Deep Fried Dumpling

Ingredients:
>Flour
>Salt to taste
>1/2 tsp Chile powder
>Coconut milk, thin

Mix together the flour, salt and Chile powder, then add sufficient coconut milk to make a paste which can be squeezed through a murukku mould or through an icing syringe with a star nozzle. Leave for 1 hour then pipe the paste onto a floured board, cut into desired lengths and make into loops.

Heat the oil and deep fry until golden. Drain and toss in salt and chile powder.

26
Chimichangas (Deep Fried Burritos)

Ingredients:
>1 lb Ground beef, browned and drained
>1 med Onion, chopped
>1/2 cup Red Chile sauce or enchilada sauce
>12 Flour tortillas
>2 cups Cheddar cheese
>2 cups Shredded lettuce
>2 cups Chopped green onions

In a large skillet, brown meat and drain. Add onion and Chile or enchilada sauce. Spoon about 3 tbsp of meat filling in center of each tortilla. Fold tortilla, tucking in ends, and fasten with wooden toothpicks. Only assemble 2 or 3 at a time as tortilla will absorb liquid from sauce.

In a deep fryer with 4 inches of oil, heat to 375F. Fry folded tortilla, turning until golden about 1 to 2 minutes. Drain on paper towels and keep warm. Garnish with cheese, lettuce, and onion.

27
Fried Soft-Shell Crab

Ingredients:
>6 ea Crabs, soft-shell
>1 cup Milk
>Pepper to taste
>Parsley, minced, fresh
>1 Egg, beaten
>Salt to taste
>Flour
>Lemon slices

1. Wash cleaned crabs well.
2. Mix egg, milk, salt and pepper; soak crabs in mixture.
3. Coat crabs with flour, then deep fry in 375F oil until brown.
4. Drain on paper towels; garnish with lemon slices and sprinkle with minced parsley.

28
Deep Fried Wonton Cookies (Teem Gok)

Ingredients:

    1 1/2 cup Chopped prunes or chopped dried apples
    1 cup chopped dried apricots
    1 1/2 cups brown sugar, packed
    1 1/2 cups flaked coconut
    1 cup chopped almonds
    24 Wonton skins

Mix together prunes, apricots, brown sugar, coconut and almonds. Place about 2 teaspoons mixture in center of each wonton skin. Moisten edges with water. Fold each skin in half to form triangle. Press edges firmly to seal.

Cover to prevent drying. Heat oil (3 to 3 1/2 inches) to 360F. Fry 3 to 4 wontons at a time, turning occasionally, until golden brown, about 1 minute on each side. Drain. Cool thoroughly and store in airtight container. Serve with ice cream or sherbet if desired.

Braised Deep Fried Pork Slices In Wine Sauce

Ingredients:
>1 tsp red rice vinegar
>2 tbs medium sherry
>3/4 cup stock
>Cornstarch paste
>1 1/2 lb boned pork butt
>3 tbs peanut oil
>3 cloves garlic, minced
>2 egg yolks
>1 tsp water
>1 cup fine plain bread crumbs

Paste:
>2 tbs cooked rice
>1/2 tsp sugar
>1 tsp dry baker's yeast
>2 tbs dark soy sauce
>2 tbs warm water
>1 tsp wet bean cheese (opt)

The flavoring of the pork with our version of Fujinese "wine lees paste" gives it a distinctive and uniquely delicious flavor.

Prepare Paste: Use mortar and pestle to pulverize cooked rice. Combine with sugar, yeast, soy and warm water. Let stand in warm place for 30 minutes to activate yeast. Authentic wine less paste is not available in the U.S. to our knowledge this is the best substitute we have found. You can add wet bean cheese for a sharper flavor.

Braise Pork: Slice pork butt across the grain into strips, 1"
by 3" by 1/2" thick. Heat peanut oil in wok until it begins to
smoke. Add some of pork to hot oil; stir-fry pieces until
they lose their pinkness; repeat in batches until all pork is
browned. Next, add garlic to wok; stir briefly. Pour in
wireless paste, rice vinegar, sherry and stock; bring to slow
boil; add pork slices. Reduce heat, cover, and simmer for
30 minutes.

Remove pork, without sauce, to large platter. Cool pork.
Cooling is essential so that it will deep-fry properly.
Reserve sauce in small pan. You can hold pork for several
hours, if you wish to braise it in advance.

Deep-fry Pork: Heat deep-frying oil. While oil is heating,
beat egg yolks with water; set out bread crumbs on platter.
Dip pork pieces in egg mixture, then into the bread crumbs,
to thoroughly cover. When oil is at deep-frying
temperature, 375 degrees, slip in a slice of pork as a test:
pork should lightly brown in about 1 minute. Place 6 pork
slices on Chinese strainer, and lower into oil, strainer and
all. Check in 2 minutes (browning should take slightly
longer than test because strainer cools the oil). If you prefer
to fry in larger batches, use more oil. Remove fried pork to
warm platter, uncovered.

Finish: Reheat sauce, and pour over pork just before
serving.

30
Fried Onion Mums Or Pom Poms

Ingredients:

> 5 yellow onions - medium to small onions or 2
> extra large onions
> 4 cups flour
> 5 tsp baking powder
> 2 tsp paprika
> 1 tsp garlic powder
> 2 tsp Greek seasonings
> 1 tsp salt or flavor to taste
> Black and/or cayenne pepper – flavor to taste
> 3 eggs
> 1 1/2 cups milk

Cut off and discard the top half-inch of the onions. Peel them but do not cut off the root and. Place each onion, root end up, on a cutting board.

With a sharp, pointed knife, make vertical cuts all around the onion about a quarter inch apart. Start the cut a quarter-inch from the root for small onions or a half-inch from the root for very large ones. Make sure the knife goes into the center of the onion. Place all the onions in a large bowl of cold water, add ice cubes, cover and refrigerate several hours or overnight. The onions will open up like mums.

Drain upside-down when ready to proceed. In a large bowl, mix together thoroughly the flour, baking powder and spices. In another bowl, beat together the eggs and milk.

Dip the onions one by one into the egg mixture, opening the petals with your fingers; let the excess drip off, and place in flour. Work the flour mixture into the center gently with fingertips. Shake off excess flour and repeat egg dip and flouring, shaking off the excess thoroughly.

Half-fill a deep fryer or large, deep, heavy pot with oil. Heat the oil to 360F. Fry the onions without crowding them – one at a time for large ones -- keeping them submerged with a spatula or by placing the frying basket on top of them. Plunge them in root end up and turn them over once. To serve at once, fry large onions for about six or seven minutes, small ones for five minutes, or until deep gold. Drain upside-down on paper towels; then invert on a serving plate. Keep warm in a low oven while frying the others.

Remove the centers of large onions with a very sharp knife. Small onions may be left whole or the center can be scooped out with a melon-ball cutter. If serving the next day, fry the onions until pale gold; do not fry completely. Let cool. When ready to serve, reheat the oil to 380F and fry the onions just long enough to heat and brown, about 15 seconds. Drain and serve. To get the same taste without making mums, simply cut onions vertically to make "petals" or crosswise and separate into rings. This can be done ahead and the petals or rings kept in ice later. Egg, flour and fry as above.

Fried Ice Cream

Ingredients:
- 1 quart vanilla ice cream
- 1/2 teaspoon ground cinnamon
- 1/2 cup sugar
- 1 cup cornflake crumbs
- 1/4 cup honey
- Whipped cream
- 4 maraschino cherries

1. Let the ice cream stand at room temperature for about 5 minutes to soften slightly.

2. Combine the cinnamon, sugar, and cornflake crumbs in a shallow pan.

3. Using an ice cream scoop, make 4 large balls of ice cream. Roll these balls in the crumb mixture to cover completely. Wrap in pieces of aluminum foil and freeze for 5 hours.

4. Heat the oil to 425F in deep fryer. As soon as it comes to heat, uncover the ice-cream balls and deep-fry very briefly-about 2 seconds. Drain momentarily and place in dessert dishes.

5. Top each ball with 1 tbs. honey, a little whipped cream, and a maraschino cherry.
Serve immediately.

32
Toffee Apples And Bananas

Ingredients:
> 2 large firm apples
> 2 firm bananas
> 2 1/4 cup flour
> 14 cup cornstarch
> 1 large egg
> 1 tsp sesame oil
> 2 tsp sesame oil
> 3/4 cup granulated sugar
> 2 tbs white sesame seeds, toasted

Peel and core the apples and cut each into 8 large wedges. Peel the bananas and cut them into 1 1/2-inch chunks. Combine the flour, cornstarch, egg and 1 teaspoon of sesame oil in a small bowl. Mix them well to form a smooth, very thick batter.

Combine the peanut oil and 2 teaspoons of sesame oil in a deep fat fryer or wok and heat the mixture until it is moderately hot. Put the fruit into the batter mixture. Then, lift out several pieces of fruit at a time with a slotted spoon and drain off any excess batter.
Deep-fry for about 2 minutes, until they are golden.
Remove with a slotted spoon and drain on paper towels.
Repeat the process until you have deep-fried all the fruit.

Just before serving, prepare a bowl of ice water filled with ice cubes. Reheat the oil over moderate heat and deep-fry the fruit a second time for about 2 minutes. Drain again on paper towels. Put the sugar, sesame seeds and 2 tablespoons of oil from the deep-frying oil into a pot. Heat the mixture until the sugar melts and begins to caramelize.

(Watch the heat to prevent it from burning.) When the caramel is light brown, add the fruit sections. Stir them gently in the caramel syrup to coat them. Then take them out and put them into the ice water to harden. Do a few at a time to prevent them from sticking together. Remove them from the water and place on a serving platter. Serve at once.

33
Khvorost (Fried Sugar Circles)

Ingredients:
       1 cup flour
       3 tbs sugar
       1 tsp cinnamon
       1/4 tsp salt
       1 egg beaten to blend
       2 1/2 tbs water
       1 tbs vodka
       1 tsp vanilla
       Cinnamon sugar

Combine flour, sugar, cinnamon and salt in medium bowl. Add egg, water, vodka and vanilla and blend well. Turn dough out onto lightly floured surface and knead 5 minutes. Cover and let rest for 15 minutes.

Roll dough out on lightly floured surface to thickness of 1/8 in. cut into strips. Cut small lengthwise slit neat 1 end of each strip. Twist opposite end of strip through opening, handling gently, to form loop.

Heat oil in deep fryer to 350F. Fry loops in batches until golden brown. Drain on paper towels. Sprinkle generously with cinnamon sugar. Serve immediately.

34
Almond Fried Ice Cream

Ingredients:
>8 scoops vanilla ice cream
>1 cup tangerine sauce
>2 cups sliced almonds

Scoop the ice cream in advance; return to freezer until extremely hard.

Heat the cooking oil in a deep fryer. Roll each ice-cream ball in the tangerine sauce then in the sliced almonds, coating thoroughly. Deep-fry for a few seconds only. Serve immediately.

35
Cranberry Fritters

Ingredients:
>   8 oz cranberry jelly, canned
>   5 tbs flour
>   1/2 tsp baking powder
>   1/2 tsp sugar
>   5 tbs water

Cranberry tartness suggests the original Chinese ingredient, a firm, gelatinous jelly flavored with the hawthorn berry (or 'shandza', which in northern China is pureed to make a delicious tart, thick, cooling drink). Enclosed within a light, deep-fried batter,
the strips of jelly become hot and soft or, in the case of cranberry, almost liquid. Buy the "jellied cranberry sauce", not the whole-berry type.

Directions:
Cut the jelly crosswise into three round slices, 1/2 inch thick. Cut each slice into three strips, approximately 1/2 x 1/2 x 2-1/2 inches. Prepare a batter by blending the flour, baking powder, sugar, and water.

Heat oil for deep-frying to 375F. Dredge the cranberry jelly strips lightly in flour, making sure all sides, including the ends, are dusted. Then dip them in the batter to coat completely, and immerse them in the oil until golden brown. Fry only a few at a time. Drain on paper toweling, and eat while hot.

36
Sichuan Dry-Fried String Beans

Ingredients:
>1 tablespoon dried shrimp
>1 tablespoon preserved sichuan
>1 pound string beans, snapped in
>1 tablespoon minced ginger
>1 tablespoon finely chopped garlic
>4 ounces ground pork butt
>1 green onion, minced
>1 teaspoon sugar
>Pinch white pepper
>2 tsp dark soy sauce
>2 tbs chicken stock
>A swirl of sesame oil

This green-bean dish is outstanding. The green beans exude aromatic flavors and have an interesting chewy texture. I do not fry the beans as long as traditional recipes call for because I want them to have some texture left.

Cover the dried shrimp with hot water for 30 minutes. Drain. Chop into the consistency of coarse bread crumbs.

Rinse the Sichuan preserved vegetables with cold water to wash off the brine and salt; chop into the same texture as the shrimp. In a deep fryer add the oil and heat to 375F.

Deep fry the beans in two or three batches for 2 to 3 minutes or until they look wrinkled, blistered and khaki color.

Remove all but 1 tablespoon of the oil from the wok. Reheat the wok over high heat.

Add the ginger and garlic; stir-fry for 15 seconds. Add the pork, preserved mustard, dried shrimp; stir-fry for 1 minute longer. Poke and break up the clumps of pork so that it looks crumbled. Add the green onion, sugar, white pepper and soy sauce; toss together to blend.

37
Fried Empanadas With Beef Or Chicken Filling

Ingredients:
>   1 kg Plain flour
>   250 g Butter, lard or margarine
>   1 Egg
>   400 ml Salted water

Beef filling:
>   150 g Butter, lard or margarine
>   2 tbs Oil
>   750 g Minced beef
>   8 Or 10 green (spring) onions
>   1 tbs Paprika
>   Salt and pepper
>   4 Hard boiled eggs, chopped
>   250 g Green olives
>   1 tsp Ground chilli
>   1/4 cup Tomato puree
>   1 tsp Ground cumin
>   1 tsp Mixed spices
>   1 tsp Cinnamon
>   1 cup Beef stock

Chicken filling:
>   500 g Minced chicken
>   3 - 4 tbs oil
>   200 g Red capsicum, finely chopped
>   300 g Onions, finely chopped
>   4 tbs Tomato puree
>   3 Hard-boiled eggs, chopped

To make dough: Sift the flour; add the melted shortening
and the egg. Add the salted water bit by bit and mix to a

firm dough. Knead for 10 minutes if making by hand, 4-5 minutes if using an electric mixer with a dough hook, or 1-2 minutes if using a food
processor with a dough hook. Leave it to rest for 15 to 30 minutes.

To make the beef filling: Heat the oil and shortening in a frying pan and sauté the green onions, finely chopped. Add the meat and stir until it is cooked. Stir in the tomato puree and remaining ingredients, cook for a few minutes more. Leave until completely cold before assembling empanadas.

To make the chicken filling: Heat the oil and fry the onions, then add the capsicum and dry until soft. Add the minced chicken and stir until it has all changed color. Season to taste, add the tomato puree, mix well and simmer for a further 3 minutes. Leave until completely cold before assembling empanadas.

Assembly and cooking: Roll out the dough about 3 mm thick and, using a saucer or something similar as a guide, cut into 24-30 circles about 14 cms in diameter. Divide whichever filling mixture you are using between the circles, putting it on one side of the circle only.

Moisten the outer rim of the dough with water and fold over into a semi-circle. Curve the ends of the folded side together a little to form a crescent, then secure the joined edges by folding them over each other in small sections to form a "rope" effect (if this sounds too confusing, just press together and decorate with a fork in the usual way).

Heat about 6-8 cm deep frying oil to very hot and deep fry the empanadas one or two at a time just until golden. Remove from the oil immediately and drain well on kitchen paper. Serve very hot.

Halve the filling ingredients or double the dough if making both beef and chicken empanadas. Empanadas often include raisins or sultanas which create an interesting flavor contrast with the meat. A handful can be added to either of these recipes if you like.

38
Original Buffalo Wings

Ingredients:
> 5 lb fresh large chicken wings
> Durkee or French's hot sauce
> Winger's original recipe hot
> Melted margarine
> Celery sticks
> Chunky blue cheese salad dressing

1. Split the wings at the joint and remove the tips. Anchor Bar has barrels of tips they use in soup stock.

2. Spread the wings out on a rack in a pan and refrigerate so they drain a minimum of 24 hours. This small step will help produce a 'crispier' final product.

3 Heat deep fryer to 350-360 degrees.

4. Fry wings in small batches until done-8-10 minutes, depending on the equipment.

5 Drain off excess oil and immediately place in large bowl and coat with hot sauce & melted margarine.

6. Serve with celery sticks and blue cheese.

NOTE: The amounts of hot sauce and margarine are really to taste. Medium 'heat' wings are approx. obtained by using 1 cup of hot sauce for the entire 5# and 1/2 cup of melted margarine. Experiment-some places do not use the melted marg. at all and just vary the volume of hot sauce to get the taste they want.

39
Onion Rings

Ingredients:
      6 - 8 medium onions
      1 cup flour
      1 cup milk
      1 egg
      1/4 teaspoon salt

Skin the onions, slice very thin, separate into rings, dip into a batter made from the flour, milk, egg, and salt, and drain well.

Heat deep fryer to 400 F. Put the onions in a wire basket, lower into the hot oil and fry until the onions are golden brown. Remove, drain on absorbent paper, sprinkle with salt, and keep hot until served.

Onions fried in this way will generally keep crisp for several days, or may be reheated in the same way as potato chips.

40
Parsley Fried Onion Rings

Ingredients:
>3/4 cup plus 2 tbs beer (not dark)
>1 cup flour
>3/4 cup finely chopped fresh parsley
>3/4 tsp Salt plus additional for
>1 large Onion
>Salsa Verde for dipping

In a bowl, whisk beer into flour until batter is smooth and whisk in parsley. Let batter stand 30 minutes and stir in 3/4 tsp salt.

Cut onion crosswise into 1/2-inch-thick slices and separate slices into rings.

In a deep fryer heat 3 inches oil to 380 F. Working in batches of 4 or 5 onion rings, drag rings through batter to coat completely, letting excess drip off, and fry, turning, until golden, about 1 to 2 minutes. With tongs, transfer rings as fried to paper towels to drain and season with additional salt.

Serve onion rings with Salsa Verde.

41
Crisp-Fried Pasta Nibbles

Ingredients:
      Pasta, in desired shapes
      Garlic salt or another seasoned salt may be used.

Cook pasta in boiling salted water until almost tender.
Drain and pat dry on paper towels.

Heat oil in deep fryer to 375F. Add pasta, a few pieces at a
time, to hot oil and fry until lightly browned and crisp.
Drain on paper towels and sprinkle with garlic salt. Serve
immediately, or cool then store in airtight container.

42
Deep Fried Okra

Ingredients:
> 8 oz Okra
> 1/2 cup Yellow corn meal
> 1/2 tsp Paprika
> 1/4 tsp Ground red pepper
> 1/4 tsp Salt
> 5 Drops hot pepper sauce
> 1 Egg
> Dipping sauces

Chunky tomato sauce: In small saucepan over medium heat, combine an 8 oz can tomato sauce, 1 small chopped onion, 1 seeded and chopped green bell pepper, 1/8 tsp chopped garlic, 1 1/2 tsp olive oil, 1/8 tsp chili powder and 1/8 tsp black pepper. Cook about 15 minutes to blend flavors.

Spicy cheese sauce: In small saucepan, over low heat, melt 1/1/2 tbs butter/margarine. Stir in 2 tbs all purpose flour; cook 5 minutes, stirring occasionally. Increase heat to medium; stir in 3/4 cup milk. Cook 5 minutes, stirring occasionally, until slightly thickened. Gradually stir in 3/4 cup shredded sharp cheddar cheese, and then stir in 4 oz can drained chopped green chilies, 1/8 tsp each ground red pepper and black pepper. Keep dipping sauces warm. In deep-fryer thermometer, heat 2 inch oil to 365 F.

Meanwhile, slice stems and tips from okra. In medium bowl, combine next five ingredients. In small dish, beat together egg and 1 tbs water. Coat okra with egg mixture. In small batches, fry coated okra until golden brown, about

1 1/2 minutes. With slotted spoon, remove to paper towel to drain. Serve immediately with warm dipping sauces.

43
Warm Springs Fried Bread

Ingredients:

    3 cups sifted all-purpose flour
    1 tbs Butter
    1 tsp Salt
    2 tbs Melted butter
    2 tsp Baking powder
    3/4 – 1 cup warm milk
    1 tsp sugar

Combine dry ingredients; cut in butter. Add enough warm milk to make soft dough, easy to handle. Knead on floured board until dough is very smooth and soft but elastic. Do not use a lot of extra flour. Divide dough into 6-8 balls and brush the tops with melted butter.

Cover and let stand 30-45 minutes. Pat out each ball into a round, 5 or 6 inches in diameter and 1/4 inch thick. Fry in deep fat (preheated to 365 F). Dough should rise immediately to surface. Cook until brown on one side, turn, and brown on other side being careful to not pierce crust. Drain on absorbent paper and serve hot.

44
Special Chicken

Ingredients:
>1 1/2 lb Chicken wings, cut-up into segments at joints.
>2 tbs Soy sauce
>1 tsp Sugar
>1 tbs Sherry wine
>A few gratings of fresh ginger
>2 tsp Hoisin sauce
>1 Clove garlic, minced
>1/4 tsp Sesame oil
>1 tsp Salt
>Dash MSG (optional)
>2 Eggs
>1/2 cup Cornstarch
>1/2 cup Flour
>Lettuce leaves, shredded
>Green onion, Chinese parsley, cashew nuts, all chopped for garnish

This is one of the better deep-fried chicken recipes I've found. It calls for chicken wings, but I used a whole chicken, cut up Chinese style and just increased the marinade ingredients a tad.

Serve this with side dishes of hoisin sauce, spiced salt (toasted salt mixed with black pepper about half and half), hot mustard and chili oil along with a bowl of finely chopped scallions. Dip piece of chicken into the dip of your choice, then into the scallions and enjoy!

Be sure to use the dark, toasted sesame oil rather than the health food store stuff.

1. Soak cut-up chicken in marinade ingredients A for 1 hour. Mix ingredients B into bowl with marinated chicken. Stir well. Will be very sticky and stiff to mix.

2. Heat 5 inches oil in deep fryer to 375F. Drop batter covered chicken piece by piece carefully into hot oil. Do not fill too full of chicken or it will take too long to brown. Should take only 5 minutes to cook through. Result will be crispy golden brown chicken pieces.

3. Drain on paper towels. Place on platter lined with lettuce shreds.

4. Garnish if desired with chopped green onions, Chinese parsley and cashew nuts.

45
Fried Banana

Ingredients:
     1 Banana, quartered
     6 tbs Water
     1/2 cup Flour
     2 tsp Double action baking
     4 tbs Honey
     Powder

Light, sweet dessert - a perfect ending to the dinner.

1. Roll the banana pieces in flour. Mix the baking soda with water to make a paste and roll the banana pieces in it.

2. Heat the oil until it is hot. Deep fry bananas for 4 minutes or until they are golden brown. Drain.

3. Pour 1 tablespoon of honey on each banana piece and serve.

46
Rick's on the Bricks Fried Dill Pickles

Ingredients:
>1 16-oz. jar hamburger dill pickles, sliced
>1 cup whole milk
>5 drops yellow food coloring (5 to 7 drops)
>3 cups flour
>Salt and pepper

Spread pickles in single layer on paper towels to drain. In small bowl, combine milk and enough yellow food coloring to produce a medium color. Place flour, salt and pepper to taste in large, shallow bowl. Set aside. To small saucepan, add enough oil to come 1 inch up the side of the pan. Heat oil to 350 F.

In small batches, submerge pickles in milk mixture. Transfer to flour bowl and roll in flour to coat all sides well. Separate slices if they stick together.

Repeat process by returning pickles to milk mixture and flour, again making sure slices are coated evenly and do not stick together.

Carefully drop one by one into hot oil and fry 3 to 5 minutes or until golden brown and crispy. Drain on paper towels. Repeat this process until all pickles are cooked. Makes 6 servings.

47
French Fried Potato Skins

Ingredients:
>   Potatoes
>   Salt
>   Garlic salt or celery salt or grated parmesan

Scrub potatoes thoroughly with brush. Using potato peeler cut off long thin spirals of skin from potatoes. (Use potatoes for another dish.) Cover skins with very cold water and let stand 30 minutes to 1 hour. Drain and carefully pat curls dry with paper towels.

Drop curls into deep oil heated to 390F and fry until golden brown and crisp, about 1 minute. Drain on paper towels and sprinkle with salt or garlic salt, celery salt or Parmesan cheese. Serve hot.

48
Cherry Dessert Wontons

Ingredients:
> 48 Premade wonton wrappers (1 package)
> 30 oz Tart cherry pie filling
> Powdered sugar or cinnamon sugar

To assemble wontons, place approximately 1 1/2 tsp cherry pie filling (2 cherries plus sauce) in the center of each wonton wrapper. Moisten the edges of each wrapper and bring one corner up over the filling to the opposite corner at an angle so that two overlapping triangles are formed. Pull the two bottom corners of the folded triangle forward so that they meet one another and slightly overlap. Moisten one end and pinch the two ends firmly together. Repeat.

Pour the oil into a deep fryer and heat to 375 F. Deep fry the wontons, 8 to 10 at a time for about two minutes or until crisp and golden. Drain on paper towels.

Fried wontons can be kept warm for about one hour in a 250 F oven or reheated for 5 minutes in a 450 F oven. Powdered sugar or cinnamon sugar can be sprinkled on the fried wontons, if desired.

49
Crispy Fried Pork And Apples

Ingredients:
>   6 Pork chops (butterflied and 1" thick)
>   1 large Apple (peeled & cored)
>   2 Eggs
>   2 tbs Half and half
>   1 cup Bread crumbs (unseasoned)
>   1 tsp Ginger (ground)
>   3/4 Salt
>   1/4 Allspice (ground)
>   1/2 tsp Coriander, ground (optional)

1. Pound each chop with a meat mallet, and slice the apple into six rings.

2. Blend the half and half and the eggs in a small bowl and then in a shallow baking dish, or on waxed paper, mix the bread crumbs, ginger, salt, (coriander, if desired), and allspice, and set aside.

3. Heat 2" to 3" of oil in a deep fryer to 350F. Dip the pork chops and the apple rings into the egg mixture, then into the bread crumbs to coat. Fry 2 pieces of pork at a time for 7 min until the crust is a deep golden brown and the pork is no longer pink in the center. Drain on paper towels.

4. Fry the apple rings for 2 to 3 min. or until they are a deep golden brown, and drain them also on the paper towels.

5. Serve one apple ring on top of each pork chop.

50
Fried Eggplant Or Zucchini

Ingredients:
> 1 cup Peeled and coarsely chopped eggplant or zucchini
> 1/2 cup All purpose flour
> 1/2 cup Dried bread crumbs (very fine)
> 1/2 cup Milk
> 1 Egg
> Powdered sugar is optional

Seasoning Mix:
> 1 1/8 tsp Salt
> 1/4 tsp Paprika
> 1/2 tsp White pepper
> 1/4 tsp Onion powder
> 1/4 tsp Garlic powder
> 1/4 tsp Ground red pepper (cayenne)
> 1/4 tsp Black pepper
> 1/4 tsp Dried thyme leaves
> 1/8 tsp Dried sweet basil leaves

Combine seasoning mix and ingredients in a small bowl, mixing thoroughly. Sprinkle the vegetables evenly with about 1/2 tsp of the mix. Place the flour in a small bowl and the breadcrumbs in another. Add 1 tsp of the seasoning mix to the flour and one tsp to the breadcrumbs, mixing each well. (Use any leftover mix to season other vegetables before cooking.) In a separate small bowl combine the milk and egg until well blended.

Heat 1 inch oil in deep fryer to 350 F. Just before frying, dredge the chopped vegetables in the seasoned flour, shaking off excess. Work quickly so flour doesn't get too moist; it's best to use your hands for this, but a slotted spoon will do. Then coat well with the milk mixture, quickly with the breadcrumbs, shaking off excess.

Place the vegetables in hot oil until dark golden brown, about 2-3 minutes, making sure to separate the vegetable pieces as you drop them into the oil. Adjust heat as necessary to keep at 350 F. Drain and serve immediately.

Sprinkle lightly with powdered sugar (If desired)

51
Fried Alligator

Ingredients:
    1 Alligator meat
    1 tsp Cayenne pepper
    1/4 cup Vinegar
    1/4 cup Flour
    1 cup Corn meal
    Salt & pepper to taste

Tenderloin fresh alligator tail, cutting pieces not to exceed 2"X 1" thick. Place in shallow dish. Pour on small amount of vinegar and add salt and pepper and cayenne to taste. Let stand for approximately 30 minutes. While gator soaks, pour into dusting bag or other container 4 parts corn meal to 1 part flour. Put about 1" oil in skillet and heat to 400 F. Roll or shake alligator strips in dusting mixture, then place in hot oil and fry until golden. Serve hot.

Suggestions: Try deep-fried Alligator nuggets as an appetizer.

52
Batter Fried Dandelion

Ingredients:
       2 cups Dandelion Blossoms
       1 Egg, beaten
       1 cup Milk
       1 cup Flour
       1/2 tsp Salt
       1/4 tsp Pepper

Pick the dandelions as close to the head as possible (the stems are very bitter). Rinse well; pat dry with paper towels. Beat the egg, milk, flour, salt, and pepper in a small bowl. Dip each flower into the batter.

Deep-fry in oil that is hot but not smoking (350F - 375F), until golden brown. Drain on paper towels and sprinkle with salt.

53
Chippewa Indian Fried Bread

Ingredients:
- 2 1/2 cups Flour
- 1 1/2 tbs Baking powder
- 1 tsp Salt
- 3/4 cup warm water
- 1 tbs Vegetable oil
- 1 tbs Nonfat dry milk powder
- Cinnamon sugar

Combine flour, baking powder and salt in large bowl. Combine water, oil and dry milk powder and stir into flour mixture until smooth dough forms. Turn out onto lightly floured surface. Knead 4 times into smooth ball. Cover and let rest 10 minutes.

Divide dough into 8 balls. Flatten with fingertips or roll out each ball to form 8- to 10-inch round. Make small hole in center of each with finger or handle of wooden spoon. Lightly flour rounds, stack and cover with towel or plastic wrap.

Heat about 1 inch of oil to 375 F in deep fryer. Gently place 1 bread round in hot oil and cook until golden and crisp, 1 to 2 minutes on each side. Drain on paper towels. Repeat with remaining dough. Serve bread hot or at room temperature, sprinkled with cinnamon sugar.

54
Fried Cucumbers

Ingredients:
- 1 Cucumber
- Salt
- Pepper
- Cracker crumbs
- 1 Egg, beaten
- Salad oil

Peel cucumber and cut lengthwise into 1/4 inch slices. Pat dry between paper towels; sprinkle with salt and pepper. Dip slices in cracker crumb, then in egg, and again in crumbs.

Deep fry in hot oil at 390 F until delicately browned. Drain on absorbent paper.

55
Fried Fragrant Bells

Ingredients:
 1 lb Ground pork
 2 Finely chopped green onions
 1 sl Minced ginger
 3 tbs Chicken broth
 1 tbs Dark soy sauce
 1 tbs Dry Sherry
 1 Egg
 2 tbs Cornstarch
 3 tbs Water
 4 Dried bean curd sheets
 Additional cornstarch
 1/4 cup Salt
 2 tbs Szechwan peppercorns

Combine pork, onion, ginger, broth, soy sauce, Sherry, egg and 1 tablespoon cornstarch in bowl and mix well. Combine remaining 1 tablespoon cornstarch with water in small bowl.

Moisten 1 bean curd sheet under running water. Place on work surface and spread with 1/4 of meat mixture. Roll as for jelly roll; brush long edge with dissolved cornstarch to seal. Repeat to make three more rolls. Cut each into slices 1 1/2 inches thick; dip each end in additional cornstarch to seal filling. (Can be done 3 to 4 hours ahead and refrigerated.)

For salt: Combine salt and peppercorns in small skillet and cook until browned. Crush in mortar with pestle.

Heat oil in deep fryer to 375 F. Add slices a few at a time and fry until crisp. Drain on paper towels. Serve hot with peppercorn salt, if desired.

56
Crispy Rattlesnake Coils

Ingredients:
    1 Rattlesnake cut in strips
    Flour
    Salt & pepper

Preparation: Cut rattlesnake into 8" strips about 1/4" thick. Salt and pepper lightly. Put flour into a container that can be covered. Add strips. Shake. Refrigerate for about two hours. This will allow the flour to become sticky.

While oil is heating in a 375 F deep fryer, pull the pieces apart and re-flour the pieces again. Add flour if necessary. When the oil is hot, add only enough snake strips so that all pieces are covered by the hot grease. Fry until golden brown. Dump into a container that has been pre-warmed in the oven. Continue frying the rest of the rattlesnake strips.

Note: The fried rattlesnake strips will appear to be coiled!

Serving: Use a basket lined with a cloth napkin. Add the fried, coiled snake pieces. Cover with the napkin.

57
Sri Lanka Fried Chiles

Ingredients:
> 24 Dried cayenne or japone chiles
> 4 tbs Salt
> 1 qt Water

Make brine from the salt and water. Soak the chilies for an hour in the brine. Heat a good quantity of oil. When it's very hot, deep fry the chilies until they are crisp. Drain, salt and serve.

This is the simplest way to fix dried chilies. I am told it is eaten as a snack at movie theaters in Sri Lanka.

58
Texas Fried Green Tomatoes

Ingredients:
>3 – 4 large Green tomatoes
>2 cups Flour
>1 tablespoon Salt
>1 tablespoon Pepper
>1 tablespoon Lawry's seasoned salt
>2 Eggs
>2 cups Milk

Cut tomatoes into almost 1/2-inch thick slices. Mix flour, salt, pepper and seasoned salt in one bowl. Mix eggs and milk in another bowl. Dip each tomato slice into the milk mixture, then into the flour, back to the milk, and then to the flour again, coating well.

Heat oil in a deep-fryer to 350 F. Add battered tomato slices a few at a time, and cook for 5 minutes, or until golden brown.

Note. Northerners can substitute cracker crumbs for flour; Southerners can use corn meal. In any case, adding a little flour will improve coverage.

59
Croquiqnolles

Ingredients:
- 1 cup Sugar
- 1/4 cup Water
- 1/2 tsp Nutmeg
- 4 Eggs
- 4 1/2 cup Flour, self-rising, sifted

1. In large mixing bowl, blend sugar and water; stir in nutmeg.

2. Beat in eggs, one at a time, and beating well after each addition.

3. Gradually blend in enough flour to make a stiff dough that can be easily handled.

4. Turn out onto lightly floured surface; divide in half.

5. Roll out each half 1/2-inch thick.

6. With floured 2 1/2-inch doughnut cutter, cut out doughnuts.

7. Heat oil to 375 F; deep-fry doughnuts until golden brown, turning once.

8. Drain thoroughly on paper towels.

9. Dust with sugar, as desired.

60
Twice-Fried Shredded Beef

Ingredients:
-Marinade-
- 3/4 lb Beef sirloin or flank steak
- 2 tbs Dry sherry
- 2 tbs Soy sauce
- 1 tsp Sugar
- 1 tsp Cornstarch
- 1 small Carrot
- 1 Green bell pepper
- 2 Ribs celery
- 1 small Onion

-Sauce-
- 2 tbs Rice vinegar
- 1 tbs Soy sauce
- 2 tsp Sesame oil
- 1 tsp Sugar
- 1/2 tsp Chili oil
- 1/2 tsp Cornstarch

Preparation: Trim and discard fat from beef. Cut beef across the grain into 1 1/2-inch matchstick pieces. Combine marinade ingredients in a medium-size bowl. Add beef; stir to coat. Set aside for 30 minutes.

Cut carrot, bell pepper, and celery into 1 1/2-inch matchstick pieces. Thinly slice onion. Set vegetables aside separately.

Combine sauce ingredients in a small bowl and set aside.

Cooking: In a deep fryer add oil to a depth of 1 1/2 to 2 inches. Place over high heat until oil reaches about 375 F. Add beef, half at a time, and deep fry for 1 minute until browned, turning occasionally. Lift out and drain on paper towels, set aside. Cook remaining beef.

Reheat oil to high heat. Add carrot and onion; cook, stirring constantly, for 1 minute. Add bell pepper and celery; fry for 1 more minute. Stir in sauce and beef. Cook until well mixed.

61
Hush Puppies

Ingredients:
> 2 cups cornmeal
> 2 teaspoons baking powder
> 1 teaspoon salt
> 1 whole onion, minced
> 2 tablespoons bacon fat
> 1 egg
> 2/3 cup milk
> 6 cups peanut oil

Mix corn meal, baking powder, salt. Sauté onion in bacon fat until just limp; cool slightly. Beat egg until light, stir in milk and onion. Stir into dry ingredients to form a stiff batter.

Heat oil in deep fryer to 350 F. Shape batter into 3" long crescents. Fry in single-layer batches in hot oil until golden brown.

62
STRUFFOLI (Honey Balls)

Ingredients:
- 3 Large eggs
- 1 tbs Butter; softened
- 1 tsp Sugar; plus
- 1/2 cup Sugar
- 2 cup All-purpose flour
- 1/2 tsp Baking powder
- 1 cup Honey
- Colored sprinkles

Whisk together: eggs, butter, and 1 tsp sugar until foamy. Add baking powder; add flour. Work the mixture into soft dough with your hands. Divide dough into 4 pieces.

On a floured surface, roll each piece into a rope about the width of your index finger and 12 inches long. Cut the ropes into 1" pieces. Toss the pieces with enough flour to dust them lightly and shake off excess flour.

Heat oil to 375 F in deep fryer. Fry the struffoli a few handfuls at a time until they puff up and are golden brown. Using a slotted spoon, transfer to a paper towel to drain.

Combine the honey and the ½ cups sugar in a large saucepan over low heat; stirring until the sugar has dissolved; keep warm over low heat. Add the fried balls, a few at a time, and turn them with a wooden spoon to coat on all sides. Transfer the balls to a large platter and mound them into a pyramid, shaping with wet hands. Sprinkle with the colored sprinkles and let stand for 1 to 2 hours. Then just break off some pieces with your hands to eat.

63
Fried Oysters

Ingredients:
      1 Doz. large oysters
      1 cup Flour with salt and pepper added
      1 Egg, beaten
      1 cup Soft bread crumbs
      Tartar sauce

Pick over the oysters carefully, pat dry in a soft cloth, and then roll in seasoned flour (flour to which a little salt and pepper have been added). Dip in beaten egg, then in crumbs. This dipping may be repeated a second time if desired and all loose crumbs should be shaken off.

Fry golden brown in deep fryer at 375 F using a frying basket and frying not more than 4 oysters at a time. Drain on soft crumpled paper toweling and serve with tartar sauce.

For Philadelphia Fried Oysters: Dip first into mayonnaise, then into crumbs after which dip them in beaten egg and crumbs and fry them in hot deep fat.

64
Fry Bread, (Baking Powder Recipe)

Ingredients:
- 1 1/2 cup Unbleached flour
- 1 cup Whole wheat flour
- 1/2 cup corn meal
- 4 tbs Baking powder
- 2 tbs Sugar
- 1/4 teaspoon salt
- 1 cup Warm milk (water can be substituted if desired)

Fry bread is one of the most popular and widespread of the modern Native American Indian foods. There are two main types of this bread that are used for everything from a quick snack to and every day dinner bread. In the North and East regions, a fried yeast bread is most popular, while in the South and west regions a recipe utilizing baking powder in lieu of yeast is the more common form. In Texas the Alabama-Coushatta use the same recipe as the Navajo Fry Bread listed below.

In a mixing bowl, sift together flour, baking powder and salt. Stir in milk and knead briefly with lightly oiled hands until smooth. Rub the remainder of the one tablespoon of oil over the dough. Cover and let sit in a warm area for about 30 minutes. Either pat or roll out enough dough to fit in the palm of your hand in a circle about one quarter inch thick. Deep fry in 350 F oil for about one minute per side or until golden brown.

Note: Dough can also be cut into triangles, squares or perfect circles if rolled out and a cookie cutter like device is used. Serve with honey, maple syrup, or as bread for meals.

65
Special Fried Peanuts

Ingredients:
    Peanuts
    Salt

Fill deep fryer with peanut oil. Heat to 375'F. Put raw
shelled peanuts in frying basket and drop down into hot oil.
When white peanuts start turning brown, take basket out
and let drip. Pour out on paper toweling; salt while hot.
After they are cool, place in airtight containers to keep
fresh.

66
KFC Chicken

Ingredients:
>3 pounds Chicken pieces
>1/2 cup Flour
>1 package Dry Italian-style salad dressing
>Salt
>1 Egg
>2 tablespoons Club soda
>1 cup Pancake mix
>1 teaspoon Poultry seasoning
>1 teaspoon Paprika
>1/4 teaspoon Pepper

Rinse chicken pieces; pat dry with paper towels. Mix flour with dry salad dressing mix & salt to taste. Dip chicken pieces in this mixture and let sit for a couple of minutes. Beat egg and club soda.

In another shallow bowl, blend pancake mix with poultry seasoning, paprika and pepper. Dip flour-coated chicken pieces in egg mixture, then in pancake mix mixture. Let sit on wire rack while heating deep fryer to 375 F.

Cook chicken pieces, turning once, until a rich golden brown, about 20-25 minutes. Drain on paper towels.] Yield: 4 servings.

Variation: To prepare Extra Crispy Chicken, dip the chicken (after it has been coated in the pancake mixture) back in the egg mixture and again in the pancake mixture. Fry until done.

67
Banana Velvet Doughnuts

Ingredients:
>2 1/2 cups Flour
>2 1/2 tsp Baking powder
>1/2 tsp Baking soda
>1/4 tsp Nutmeg
>1/2 tsp Salt
>2 Eggs
>1/2 cup Honey
>1 Banana
>2 tbs Butter or margarine
>1/2 cup Sour cream
>1/2 tsp Vanilla

Sift together dry ingredients. Beat eggs until light. Add honey gradually and continue beating until well mixed. Beat in mashed banana, butter, sour cream and vanilla. Stir in flour mixture. (Dough should be soft.) Chill 2 hours or longer. Roll out on floured board about 1/4-inch thick. Cut with doughnut cutter.

In deep fryer heated to 370 F, fry a few at a time. (Fry the holes as well as the doughnuts.) Turn doughnuts when they rise to the surface and are brown on the underside. Fry until brown on both sides. Remove from fat and drain thoroughly.

Note: May form into long rolls and twist together to form crullers, cutting off every 2 inches.

68
Fried Crawfish Tails

Ingredients:
-Crawfish-
   1 lb Crawfish tails, peeled and deveined
   1/2 cup Sherry
   1 1/2 cup Flour
   2 large Eggs
   1 pinch Salt
   12 oz Beer, dark
   1 dash Pepper, cayenne
   Pepper (to taste)
   Salt (to taste)

-Sauce-
   2 large Egg yolks
   1 tbs Juice, lemon
   1/2 tsp Mustard, dry
   1/4 tsp Sauce, Worcestershire
   1 dash Tabasco
   3/4 cup Oil
   1 tbs Water, hot
   1 tbs Sherry
   1 tsp Chives, minced
   1 tsp Ketchup
   1 dash Pepper, cayenne
   Pepper (to taste)
   Salt (to taste)

Crawfish: Marinate the tails in sherry for an hour or more.
Meanwhile, mix the cup of flour, eggs, salt and cayenne
until smooth and slowly add beer to make the batter the
consistency of pancake batter. Drain tails and roll in

remaining flour. Shake off excess and dip in batter. Fry in hot oil until golden.

Sauce: Beat the yolks with lemon juice, mustard, Worcestershire and Tabasco. Slowly drizzle in oil to form mayonnaise base. Add hot water to stabilize the sauce. Fold in remaining ingredients and correct seasoning. Serve with hot crawfish tails.

69
Fried Rabbit In Breadcrumbs

Ingredients:
>3 tbs Milk
>1 oz Flour
>1/4 tsp Salt
>1/4 tsp Black pepper
>1 4 lb rabbit, cleaned and cut into serving pieces
>1 Egg -- lightly beaten with 1 tsp Water
>3 oz Fresh breadcrumbs
>4 Parsley sprigs

Place milk in one bowl and mix together flour, salt and pepper in another. Dip rabbit in milk then flour mixture, coating thoroughly. Set aside for 10 minutes.

Combine egg and water in one bowl and breadcrumbs in another. Dip rabbit first in egg mixture, then in breadcrumbs, coating thoroughly. Fill deep fryer one third full with oil and heat until it reaches 360 F.

Fry the rabbit pieces for 20 minutes or until tender when pierced with a fork. Remove from pan and drain on paper towels. Arrange on a serving dish garnish with parsley sprigs and serve immediately.

This can be served with sautéed potatoes and any fresh green vegetables.

70
Salvation Army Doughnuts

Ingredients:
  2 tbs Vegetable shortening
  1 cup Sugar
  2 Eggs, beaten
  4 3/4 Flour
  2 tsp Baking powder
  1 tsp Salt
  3/4 Milk
  1/2 Nutmeg
  1/2 tsp Vanilla extract

Mix shortening and sugar until fluffy. Add eggs and vanilla if using extract and beat well. Combine dry ingredients (including vanilla if using powder) then sift together. Add dry mixture to creamed mixture, alternating with milk.

Roll dough 1/2 inch thick on floured board. Cut into rounds, and cut out centers. A glass works well for cutting, with a small, empty prescription pill bottle to cut the centers. The centers can be rolled together for more doughnuts or fried as they are for 'donut holes.'

Deep fry in hot oil, turning once until browned. Drain on grocery bag (to absorb oil) and dust with confectioner's sugar. Yield: depends on how thin you roll, and what you do with the centers.

71
Corn Dogs

Ingredients:
  6 Frankfurters
  1/2 cup Yellow corn meal
  1 cup Sifted all-purpose flour
  1 teaspoon Salt
  1/4 teaspoon Baking powder
  1 cup Milk
  1 large Egg

Pat frankfurters dry and set aside. In a bowl whisk together the corn meal, flour, salt, and baking powder. In a small bowl whisk together the milk and egg until combined. Add the milk mixture into the dry ingredients, whisking until smooth.

In a deep fryer heat 3 to 4 inches of oil to 375 F. Dip a frankfurter in the batter and coat completely. Fry until browned about 2 to 3 minutes. Two to three frankfurters can be fried at a time. Transfer to paper towels to drain. Allow oil to return to appropriate temperature and fry remaining frankfurters in same manner.

72
Coconut Fried Ice Cream

Ingredients:
>1 qt Vanilla ice cream
>2 Eggs, beaten
>1/2 tsp Vanilla extract
>4 cups Coconut flavored cookie crumbs
>1/2 cup Coconut, flaked

Place 8 scoops of ice cream on a cookie sheet; freeze at least 1 hour or until firm.

Combine eggs and vanilla; mix well, and divide in half. Cover half of egg mixture and chill. Combine cookie crumbs and coconut; divide mixture in half. Set half of crumb mixture aside.

Dip each ice cream ball in egg mixture, and dredge in crumbs mixture. Place on a cookie sheet, and freeze at least 1 hour or until firm. Remove from freezer; dip in remaining egg mixture, and dredge in remaining crumb mixture. Return to cookie sheet; cover and freeze several hours or until firm. Fry ice cream balls in deep fryer at 375 F for 30 seconds or until golden brown. Drain on paper towels, and serve immediately.

73
Deep Fried Cherries

Ingredients:
- 1 lb Fresh ripe red cherries
- 1 cup Flour, all purpose
- 1/4 cup Sugar
- 1/3 cup Milk
- 1/3 cup Dry white wine
- 3 Eggs
- Confectioner's sugar
- Cinnamon

Fresh fruit coated with batter and deep fried is a favorite dessert in several eastern European countries. Plums, apples or currants are prepared in the same manner. In Hungary this dessert is called "Cseresznye Kisutve".

Wash cherries and wipe dry. Do not remove stems. Tie with thread to form clusters of 4 cherries. Combine flour, sugar, milk, wine and eggs in a bowl. Mix to make a smooth batter. Dip each cluster of cherries into batter, coating well.

Drop into deep fryer heated to 375 F. When golden, remove with a slotted spoon and drain. Serve at once with confectioner's sugar and cinnamon.

Deep Fried Mozzarella Cubes

Ingredients:

    Pizza Sauce
    1 tablespoon Olive oil
    1/3 cup Finely chopped onion
    1 clove Garlic, crushed in press
    1 cup Tomato sauce
    1/4 cup Water
    1 teaspoon dried Oregano
    1/2 teaspoon dried Basil
    1/4 teaspoon Hot red pepper flakes
    Mozzarella Cubes
    1 pound Mozzarella cheese, cut in 36 1" cubes
    1/2 cup All-purpose flour
    3 large Eggs, beaten
    3/4 cup Italian bread crumbs
    10 strands Spaghetti, broken into 36 3-inch lengths

To make the sauce: In a small saucepan over medium heat, heat the oil. Add the onion and cook, stirring occasionally, until golden, about 4 minutes. Add the garlic and cook until fragrant, about 1 minute. Stir in the tomato sauce, water, oregano, basil, and red pepper flakes. Bring to a simmer and reduce heat to low. Simmer until slightly thickened, about 10 minutes. Set aside and keep warm. (The sauce can be prepared up to 1 day ahead, covered, and refrigerated. Reheat before serving.)

To make the cubes: Heat 2 - 3 inches of oil in deep fryer to 365 F.

Place the flour in a shallow bowl. Beat the eggs in another shallow bowl. Place the bread crumbs in a third shallow bowl. One at a time, roll each mozzarella cube in the flour, dip in the eggs, then coat completely with the bread crumbs. Set aside on the waxed paper.

Deep-fry the spaghetti until golden brown, about 2 minutes. Using a wire-mesh skimmer, transfer to the paper towels to drain and cool. In batches, without crowding, deep fry the mozzarella cubes until golden brown, about 3 minutes. Using the skimmer, transfer to the paper towels and keep warm in the oven while frying the rest.

To serve, spear each cube with a spaghetti stick. Serve immediately with a bowl of the warm sauce for dipping. Makes 36 cubes. (4 to 6 appetizer servings)

75
Tuna Croquettes

Ingredients:
>   2 tablespoons Butter
>   1/4 cup All-purpose flour
>   3/4 teaspoon Salt
>   1/8 teaspoon Pepper
>   1 cup Milk
>   2 cans (7 ounces each) Tuna, drained
>   2 tablespoons Chopped parsley
>   1/2 teaspoon Lemon juice
>   Fine dry bread crumbs
>   1 Egg, lightly beaten
>   2 tablespoons Water

In medium saucepan, melt butter. Add flour, salt and pepper; mix well. Gradually add milk and cook until thick, stirring constantly. Stir in tuna, parsley and lemon juice; mix well then chill. Shape mixture into 8 croquettes; roll in crumbs, dip into slightly beaten egg mixed with water and roll again in crumbs.

Fry in small batches in deep fryer at about 370 F for about 5 minutes. Croquettes should be golden brown. Transfer tuna croquettes to paper towels to drain.

76
Crispy Potato Skins

Ingredients:

    4 large Baking potatoes, scrubbed
    Salt
    Pepper
    Sour cream mixed with chives, optional
    Shredded cheese, optional

Prick potatoes in several places with a fork; bake in a 400 F oven until tender, about 1 hour. Remove, cool slightly, and cut in halves lengthwise. Scoop out potatoes and refrigerate for another meal or casserole topping.

Cut skins in half again. Heat oil in a deep fryer to 375 F. Place potato skins in deep fryer basket; lower into oil and deep fry for about 2 to 3 minutes or until skins are browned and crisp.

Transfer potato skins to paper towels to drain. Sprinkle with salt and pepper. Serve with sour cream and chives, if desired, or top with cheese and place under the broiler to melt.

77
Deep Fried Liver Strips

Ingredients:
>1 pound Calf liver
>1 teaspoon Salt
>1 teaspoon Dried leaf oregano
>Dash pepper
>1/4 cup Olive oil
>2 tablespoons Lemon juice
>Lemon wedges (optional)
>Parsley (optional)

Cut liver into strips, 2-1/2 x 1/2 inch, and put into a bowl; sprinkle with salt, oregano and pepper. Add olive oil and lemon juice. Stir to coat liver. Cover and refrigerate 2 hours or longer.

Heat oil in deep fryer to 365 F. Remove livers from marinade. Fry several strips at a time in hot oil for 20 to 30 seconds or until brown. Serve immediately garnished with lemon wedges and parsley, if desired.

78
Farmhouse Fried Pork And Apples

Ingredients:
      6 boneless Loin pork chops, 1/2 inch thick
      1 large Apple, peeled and cored
      2 Eggs, slightly beaten
      2 tablespoons Milk
      1 cup Unseasoned dry bread crumbs
      1 teaspoon Ginger
      3/4 teaspoon Salt
      1/2 teaspoon Ground coriander (optional)
      1/4 teaspoon Allspice

Pound each chop to 1/4 inch thickness with meat mallet. Slice apple into 6 rings. Combine eggs and milk in shallow bowl or pie plate. Mix well. Dip pork and apple rings in egg mixture. Coat with crumbs.

Fry pork and apple rings, a few at a time, in oil heated to 365°F. Fry 2 or 3 minutes until deep golden brown. Turn as needed for even browning. Drain on paper towels

79
Chicken Kiev

Ingredients:

       4 large Whole chicken breasts, skinned and boned
       1 teaspoon Salt
       1/3 cup Butter or margarine
       1 tablespoon Minced parsley
       1 teaspoon Lemon juice
       1 clove Garlic, minced
       1/3 cup All-purpose flour
       1-1/2 cups Dry bread crumbs
       2 Eggs, lightly beaten

Cut chicken breasts in half and sprinkle with salt. Mix butter, parsley, lemon juice and garlic. Spread 2 teaspoons along the center length of each chicken breast half. Tuck in ends and long sides around flavored butter; skewer or tie to close.

Place flour and bread crumbs in separate flat dishes; beat eggs in a shallow bowl. Dip prepared chicken breast first in flour, then eggs, and then crumbs. Place seam-side down on a plate; refrigerate for at least 2 hours or until crumbs are set.

Heat 2 inches oil in deep fryer to 365 F. Fry chicken rolls in hot Crisco for 5 minutes or until done. Remove with slotted spoon. Serve immediately with brown rice.

80
Fish Sticks - Taco Style

Ingredients:
>   1 package (9 ounces) Frozen fish sticks
>   1/4 cup Taco sauce
>   1/2 cup Shredded Monterey Jack cheese

Heat oil to 365 F in deep fryer. Fry frozen fish sticks in hot oil for 3 minutes or until browned. Drain on paper towels.

Arrange fried fish sticks on a broiler plate. Drizzle taco sauce over fish sticks; sprinkle with cheese. Broil 4 inches from heat for 1 to 2 minutes or until cheese is melted

81
Pineapple Drumsticks

Ingredients:
>1 Egg, slightly beaten
>1/4 cup Water
>2 tablespoons Milk
>1/4 cup All-purpose flour
>1 tablespoon Cornstarch
>1 tablespoon Cornmeal
>1/8 teaspoon Baking powder
>12 Broiler-fryer chicken drumsticks

-Pineapple Sauce -
>1 cup Green pepper chunks
>1/2 cup Coarsely chopped onion
>1 tablespoon Crisco all-vegetable shortening or 1 tablespoon Crisco Stick
>1 can (20 ounces) Pineapple chunks in pineapple juice, drained; reserve juice
>2/3 cup Cider vinegar
>1/2 cup packed Brown sugar
>2 tablespoons Soy sauce
>4 teaspoons Cornstarch
>2 tablespoons Water

Combine egg, water, and milk. Combine flour, 1 tablespoon cornstarch, cornmeal, and baking powder; add to first mixture and mix until smooth. Dip each drumstick into batter and let excess batter drain for a couple of seconds.

Heat oil to 350 F in deep fryer. Fry drumsticks in hot oil for 14 to 16 minutes or until chicken is crisp, brown, and tender. Remove with slotted spoon and place on paper towels.

While chicken is frying prepare sauce. Melt 1 tablespoon Crisco in a saucepan. Sauté green pepper and onion for 3 to 4 minutes or until crisp-tender. Add reserved pineapple juice, vinegar, brown sugar, and soy sauce. Mix cornstarch into water. Add to sauce until blended, stirring constantly. Add pineapple chunks. Bring to boiling, stirring occasionally. Cook for 2 minutes.

Spoon half of sauce over fried drumsticks. Serve with cooked rice and remaining sauce.

82
Deep Fryer Monte Cristo Sandwich

Ingredients:
> 12 slices White bread
> 8 slices Gruyère cheese
> 1/2 lb. sliced Cooked ham
> 1 tbs plus 1 tsp Prepared mustard
> 1/2 lb. Sliced cooked chicken breast
> Toothpick
> 4 Eggs, beaten
> 3/4 cup Milk

Heat oil in deep fryer to 400 F. Place a slice of cheese on a slice of bread and top with ham slice. Spread with mustard and top with another piece of bread. Cover with another slice of cheese, chicken and last piece of bread.

Cut triple decker sandwich into quarters and secure with toothpicks. Combine egg and milk in a bowl. Dip sandwich quarters into egg mixture, coating all sides.

Deep fry 3-4 minutes until golden. Drain on absorbent paper. Remove toothpicks before serving.

83
Deep Fried Cinnamon Funnel Cakes

Ingredients:

       2 cups All purpose flour
       2 tbs Sugar
       1 tsp Baking powder
       1 tsp Ground cinnamon
       1/4 tsp Salt
       2 Eggs, lightly beaten
       1 1/4 cups Milk
       1 cup Powdered sugar

Heat oil in deep fryer to 375 F. Combine next 5 ingredients in a mixing bowl. Combine beaten eggs and 1 cup milk in another bowl. Stir into flour mixture until smooth. If batter is too thick, stir in additional milk.

Fry one cake at a time. Holding finger over funnel spout, pour about 1/3 cup of batter into funnel. Hold funnel over preheated oil and release finger. Using a circular pattern, pour batter into fryer. Fry about 1-1/2 minutes until golden. Turn and fry another 1-1/2 minutes.

Transfer cake to absorbent paper to drain. Sprinkle with powdered sugar. Repeat process until batter is used. Serve warm. Alternately: Batter may be slowly poured into hot oil from a glass measuring cup.

84
Deep Fryer Corn Fritters

Ingredients:
>3 large Eggs
>1/2 cup Unsalted butter, melted
>1/2 cup Milk
>2/3 cup All purpose flour
>1 tbs plus 2 tsp Baking powder
>1/2 cup Brown sugar
>1/4 tsp Salt
>1 lb. Corn, thawed if frozen, drained
>7 ounces Canned creamed corn

Combine eggs, butter and milk in a bowl and beat with an electric mixer on medium speed. Add next 4 ingredients and mix thoroughly. Beat in remaining ingredients on low speed.

Heat oil in deep fryer to 370 F. Gently drop large spoonfuls of batter into fryer. Do not crowd. Fry and turn occasionally until golden on all sides. Drain on absorbent paper towel.

85
Calabash-Style Flounder

Ingredients:

       5-1/4 Flounder fillets, skinned, about 6 ounces each
       2/3 cup Milk
       1/2 cup Buttermilk baking mix
       1/2 cup White cornmeal
       3/4 Lemon, cut in wedges
       5-1/4 Sprigs parsley

Place flounder fillets in a shallow baking dish. Pour in enough milk to cover. Marinate 15 minutes. Combine baking mix and cornmeal in a bowl. Toss with a fork to blend.

Heat 2 inches of oil in deep fryer at 365 F. Drain fish from milk mixture. Dredge each fillet in cornmeal mixture, coating well on both sides. Shake off excess. Add fillets to hot oil and deep-fry about 4 minutes, turning once, until golden brown and crisp on both sides. Take care to maintain correct oil temperature.

Drain on paper towels and serve hot, garnished with lemon wedges and parsley sprigs.

86
Deep Fryer Apple Dumplings

Ingredients:
>   1/4 cup Unsalted butter
>   6 Granny Smith apples, peeled, cored and cut into
>   bite-sized pieces
>   1/4 cup Brown sugar
>   1 tsp Ground cinnamon
>   1 tsp Lemon zest
>   10 Wonton wrappers
>   1/4 cup Confectioner's sugar

Melt butter in a heavy nonstick skillet over medium heat.
Sauté apples and next 3 ingredients, stirring occasionally,
until softened. Transfer to a bowl and chill well.

Place about 1/4 cup of apple mixture in the center of each
wonton wrapper. Moisten edges of wrapper with water and
bring corners to the top, forming a point, and press firmly.
Repeat with remaining wrappers and filling.

Heat oil in deep fryer to 375 F. Add dumplings to fry
basket 2 at a time. Lower into hot oil and fry until golden.
Drain on absorbent paper and serve hot sprinkled with
confectioner's sugar.

87
Jalapeño Kickers

Ingredients:

> 10 to 12 fresh Jalapeño peppers or 1 (3 1/2-ounce)
> can jalapeño peppers
> Cream Cheese
> 1/2 cup Flour
> 1 Egg
> 1/2 cup Milk
> 2 tablespoons Bread crumbs
> 1/4 teaspoon Onion salt
> 1/8 teaspoon Garlic salt
> 1/4 teaspoon Vegetable oil
> 1/4 cup Flour
> 1 teaspoon Sugar

CAUTION: Wear plastic gloves when working with peppers. Do not touch eye area.

To prepare fresh jalapeño peppers: rinse, cut in half lengthwise, remove seeds and stems, place in boiling water and remove after 2 minutes; drain well. To prepare canned jalapeño peppers: drain, cut in half lengthwise, and remove seeds and stems.

Fill each pepper half with cream cheese until slightly rounded. Place 1/2 cup flour in separate bowl, set aside. In a second bowl, beat egg with milk. In a third bowl, prepare breading by combining bread crumbs, onion salt, garlic salt and oil. Stir in flour and sugar until mixed thoroughly. Roll each pepper in flour, dip in egg mixture and then cover with breading. For a heavier breading, dip in egg mixture again and cover with breading a second time. Gently set aside until ready to deep fry.

Deep fry in 375 F heat for approximately 1 to 2 minutes or until golden brown. (Tip: Remove immediately if cream cheese filling appears through the coating.) Place fried peppers on paper toweling. Serve warm. If desired, serve with salsa.

88
Curried Chicken Squares

Ingredients:

    18 slices Soft white bread
    3 tablespoons Soft bread crumbs
    1 (5-ounce) can Chunk white chicken or 3/4 cup minced cooked chicken
    1/4 cup Roasted shelled Virginia type peanuts
    1/4 cup Minced green onion
    1/8 teaspoon 5-spice powder or Allspice
    1 teaspoon Curry powder
    1/4 teaspoon Sugar
    Dash pepper
    1 teaspoon Soy sauce
    2 tablespoons Chopped parsley
    1 Egg yolk, slightly beaten

Remove crusts from bread; cover with a damp towel or plastic wrap to keep soft. Make crumbs from crusts by putting a few at a time into a blender. Combine 3 tablespoons bread crumbs with chicken, peanuts, green onion, 5-spice powder, curry powder, sugar, pepper, soy sauce, and parsley; mix well. Roll bread slices very thin with a rolling pin. Cut each square in half; place a teaspoon of chicken mixture on each piece. Brush edges of bread with egg yolk; fold in half to form a square. Pinch to seal and trim if necessary.

In deep fryer at 380 F, fry 3 or 4 at a time, turning once until desired brownness is reached (about 2 minutes). Remove from oil and drain on absorbent paper. Repeat until all squares are cooked. May be served with mustard sauce.

89
Ole' Virginia Peanut Chicken Bites

Ingredients:
>1 1/2 cups Finely chopped roasted shelled
>Virginia type peanuts
>1/4 cup Cornstarch
>1/2 teaspoon Sugar
>1/4 teaspoon Powdered ginger
>2 tablespoons Lemon juice
>2 Egg whites, lightly beaten
>2 Whole chicken breasts, skinned and boned

Put chopped peanuts in a 9-inch pie plate. In a small bowl, combine cornstarch, sugar, and ginger; blend in lemon juice and egg whites. Cut chicken into thin slices. Dip slices in egg mixture, and then roll in peanuts to coat.

Cook 3 or 4 Chicken Bites at a time in deep fryer until desired brownness is reached (about 2 minutes), turning once. Remove from oil, and drain on absorbent paper. Repeat until all Bites are cooked. May be served with peach sauce.

90
Chili Cheese Balls (Mexican Tidbit)

Ingredients:
>3 tablespoons chopped Jalapeno chilies
>1 (8-ounce) packaged grated Parmesan cheese
>1 (8-ounce) package Cream cheese
>2 Egg yolks
>1/2 cup chopped roasted shelled Virginia type
>peanuts
>Bread crumbs

Mix chilies, cheeses, and egg yolks together until well blended; add peanuts. Form into 1-inch balls. Roll in bread crumbs; refrigerate.

Cook 3 or 4 at a time in deep fryer, until they float in oil and desired brownness is reached (about 2 minutes). Remove from oil and drain on absorbent paper. Repeat until all cheese balls are cooked.

91
Beignets (New Orleans-Style Square Donuts)

Ingredients:
> 1 (1-pound) package Hot Roll Mix
> 1/4 cup Sugar
> 1 teaspoon Vanilla
> Confectioners' sugar, sifted

Prepare roll mix according to package directions, adding 1/4 cup sugar to flour mixture and vanilla to hot water. When kneading is completed, proceed as follows: Coat a bowl with shortening or oil; roll ball of dough in bowl to coat with oil. Cover with waxed paper and a towel. Refrigerate for several hours or overnight.

Remove dough from refrigerator; punch down and cut in half. On a lightly floured surface, roll each half to make a 9- x 2inch rectangle. Cut each into 12 (3-inch) squares. Cover with a towel and let rise for 30 minutes.

Deep fry beignets, two at a time, in deep fryer at 375 F. Fry 1 1/2 minutes; turn and fry 1 1/2 minutes or until golden brown. Sprinkle generously with confectioners' sugar.

92
Bowties

Ingredients:
>2 cups Flour, plus extra for rolling
>1/3 cup Confectioners' sugar, plus extra for dusting
>4 tablespoons Unsalted butter, chilled, cut into small pieces
>1 Egg plus 3 egg yolks
>1/4 cup Sour cream
>2 teaspoons Lemon juice
>3 to 4 teaspoons Grated lemon peel, or to taste

In medium bowl, sift together flour and confectioners' sugar. Cut in chilled butter until mixture is sandy looking. Add egg and yolks, sour cream, lemon juice and lemon peel. Gently mix with fork until just combined.

Turn dough onto lightly floured surface and gently knead until dough is smooth. Form into 2 disks, wrap in plastic wrap and refrigerate for about 1 hour.

Preheat oil in deep fryer. Using only as much flour as necessary, roll one disk out no more than 1/8-inch thick. With a pastry wheel, cut dough into 2- by 4-inch rectangles. Make a 3/4-inch diagonal slit in center. Pull one end through slit and gently pull as far as it will go without tearing. Let sit about 10 minutes before frying. Repeat with second disk. Again let bowties sit about 10 minutes before frying. Fry a few at a time until golden on both sides, turning carefully as needed. Do not overcook. Drain on paper towels. Dust with confectioners' sugar when cool.

Rose Variation: Using fluted or plain biscuit cutters, cut circles of three different sizes. Put the circles one on top of the other, with the smallest on top. Pinch together securely in the middle, forcing the circles to bend upward. Let sit for about 10 minutes before frying. Carefully place in oil. Using a wooden spoon, gently hold under the oil to brown. Drain on paper towels. Dust with confectioners' sugar and place a drop of jam in the center.

93
Buñuelos

Ingredients:

       2 cups All-purpose flour
       1 teaspoon Baking powder
       1/2 teaspoon Salt
       1 tablespoon Sugar
       2 teaspoons Anise seeds, pulverized or ground in a spice grinder
       1 Egg
       1/2 cup Milk
       2 tablespoons Unsalted butter, melted
       1/2 cup Sugar
       1 tablespoon Anise seed, pulverized
       2 teaspoons Ground coriander
       1 teaspoon Ground cinnamon
       1/4 teaspoon Ground cloves

In medium bowl, sift together flour, baking powder, salt, sugar and ground anise. In a second bowl, whisk together egg, milk and butter. Stir into flour mixture until combined. On a lightly floured surface, gently knead until dough is smooth and elastic. Shape into balls about 1 1/2 inches in diameter. Cover and let rest 15 to 30 minutes. (Dough may be refrigerated overnight, if necessary.) Preheat oil in deep fryer to 380 F.

Roll each ball of dough into a thin disk, about 4 to 5 inches wide. Fry one disk at a time, until golden, about 2 minutes, turning frequently. Drain on paper towels. Sift sugar, anise, coriander, cinnamon and cloves together. Sprinkle Bunñuelos with spiced sugar mixture while still warm and serve.

94
Cardamom Funnel Cakes

Ingredients:
- 2 cups All-purpose flour
- 2 tablespoons Sugar
- 1 teaspoon Baking powder
- 1 teaspoon Ground cardamom
- 1/4 teaspoon Salt
- 2 Eggs, lightly beaten
- 1 to 1 1/4 cups Milk

Combine flour, sugar, baking powder, cardamom, and salt in a mixing bowl. Combine beaten eggs and 1 cup milk; pour into flour mixture and stir until smooth. If batter is too heavy, add additional milk. Batter should pour in a heavy stream.

Pour about 1/3 cup of batter into funnel. (Hold finger over end as funnel is filled.) Hold funnel over preheated oil in deep fryer; release finger and let batter pour into fryer in a circular pattern. Fry 1 1/2 minutes; turn and fry another 1 1/2 minutes. Fry one cake at a time. Continue until all batter is used. Serve warm with powdered sugar or syrup.

95
Sufganiyot

Ingredients:
>   3/4 cup Orange juice
>   1/2 cup Margarine
>   1/4 cup Sugar
>   2 packages Dry yeast
>   3 1/2 cups Flour
>   2 Eggs, beaten
>   Dash of salt
>   1 cup Sugar
>   1 tablespoon Cinnamon

In small saucepan, combine juice, margarine and sugar. Heat until margarine melts and ingredients are blended. Cool the mixture until it is lukewarm. Add yeast to mixture in saucepan and stir until dissolved. In large bowl, combine flour, eggs and salt. Add to juice-yeast mixture. Mix well.

Turn dough onto lightly floured surface and knead until dough is smooth and elastic. Place dough in greased bowl, cover with a cloth and let rise in a warm place for 1 to 1 ½ hours.

Punch down. On lightly floured surface, roll dough to 1/2-inch thickness and cut doughnuts using a 2-inch cutter. Place doughnuts on waxed paper about 1 inch apart and let rise for another 30 to 45 minutes. Preheat oil in deep fryer to 385 F. Fry in hot oil, a few at a time, until golden. Drain well on paper towels. Combine 1 cup sugar and 1 tablespoon cinnamon in a plastic bag and shake well. Then add fried doughnuts, a few at a time, and shake until each is coated with the mixture.

96
Lithuanian Fried Cookies

Ingredients:
> 6 Egg yolks
> 6 tablespoons Dairy sour cream
> 1 teaspoon Vanilla
> 1 teaspoon Grated lemon peel
> Dash salt
> 1 1/4 cups All-purpose flour
> 2 tablespoons Flour

Beat egg yolks, sour cream, vanilla, lemon peel, and salt together until well mixed. Add 1 1/4 cups flour, stirring to form soft dough. Sprinkle 1 tablespoon flour on pastry cloth or other surface. Turn dough out onto floured surface. Sprinkle remaining flour over surface.

Pat and roll dough to form a 16- x 15-inch square. Let stand a few minutes before cutting. Make 8 cuts (2-inches apart) across 16-inch sides. Make 5 cuts across the 15-inch side. You will have 42 (2- x 3-inch) rectangles. Cut these each diagonally to make 84 triangles. Make a slit in the center of the widest end; pull the other end through.

In deep fryer, cook 3 or 4 at a time, turning once, until desired brownness is reached (about 2 minutes). Remove from oil and drain on absorbent paper. Repeat until all cookies are cooked.

Batter Fried Oriental Dinner

Ingredients:
    1 Egg
    3/4 cup Ice Water
    1 cup All-purpose flour
    2 to 3 tablespoons Chinese Seasoning Mix
    2 Turkey, pork or beef cutlets OR 10 cleaned and
    shelled green shrimp
    Salt and pepper
    12 or 16 assorted Mushrooms, pepper strips, pea
    pods, eggplant slices OR squash slices
    Or 2-inch pieces of Asparagus
    2 cups Cooked rice

Preheat oil in deep fryer 385 F. Beat together eggs, ice water, flour and seasoning; mix until smooth. Add an ice cube or two to keep mixture cool. Sprinkle meat with salt and pepper and cut into thin strips. Select an assortment of vegetables.

Dip meat and vegetables into batter a few at a time. Fry 2 to 4 minutes or until golden brown. To serve, arrange an assortment of vegetables and meat on plate with a scoop of rice. If desired, serve with Mahogany Dip (below) and soy sauce.

98
Mahogany Dip

Ingredients:
> 1 8-ounce can Jellied cranberry sauce
> 1/4 cup Orange marmalade
> 1 tablespoon Soy sauce
> 1 tablespoon Wine vinegar
> 1/2 teaspoon Dry mustard
> Sprinkle of Dried red pepper flakes

Combine all ingredients in a small saucepan.

Heat, stirring, until cranberry sauce and marmalade are melted. Serve warm or cold.
Makes about 1 cup

99
Veggie Fritters with Thai Peanut Sauce

Ingredients:
>1 cup All-purpose flour
>1 tablespoon Baking powder
>1/4 teaspoon Salt
>5 teaspoons Vegetable oil
>2/3 cup Cold water
>4 cups Asparagus tips, broccoli, cauliflowerettes, carrot sticks, pea pods, zucchini slices, or mushrooms
>Thai Peanut Sauce (Recipe below)

Combine flour, baking powder, and salt in bowl. Stir in oil and mix until a loose ball is formed. Add water gradually, mixing until a stiff batter is formed. Blanch asparagus, broccoli, cauliflower, and carrots (zucchini and mushrooms do not have to be blanched) by dipping them into boiling water for 1 minute; drain and cool under cold running water.
Dry on paper towels. Dip vegetables into batter, allowing excess to drip off.

Cook 3 or 4 at a time, until they float in oil and desired brownness is reached (about 2 minutes). Remove from oil and drain on absorbent paper. Repeat until all vegetables are cooked. Makes about 1 1/3 cups batter

Thai Peanut Sauce
>2 tablespoons Finely chopped onions
>3/4 cup Roasted shelled Virginia-type peanuts
>1/4 cup Shredded coconut
>3/4 cup Water
>1/2 teaspoon Garlic powder

2 teaspoons Brown sugar
1/4 to 1/2 teaspoon Cayenne
2 tablespoons Soy sauce
2 tablespoons Lemon juice

Put onions, peanuts, coconut, water, garlic powder, sugar, and Cayenne in a blender container; blend until almost smooth. Pour into a small sauce pan. Cook and stir until mixture boils and thickens. Serve warm or cold. Makes about 1 cup

100
Deviled Egg Roll Ups

Ingredients:
    6 hard Cooked eggs
    3 tablespoons Mayonnaise
    2 teaspoons Dijon mustard
    2 teaspoons Minced pimiento
    1/2 teaspoon Minced dill or chives
    12 Phyllo dough sheets
    1 Egg white, lightly beaten

Cool eggs and peel. Cut in half lengthwise and carefully remove yolks. Set white aside. Mash yolks and mix with remaining ingredients, except phyllo dough and egg white. Fill cooked egg whites with mixture; cover and chill. Cut each filled half egg in half lengthwise to make 24 pieces.

Working quickly, fold 1 sheet of phyllo dough into quarters; cut in half. Place one deviled egg piece at one end. Brush sides with lightly beaten egg whites. Roll phyllo strip to enclose egg. Twist ends to close. Keep dough and wrapped eggs covered with plastic or a damp cloth as you work. In deep fryer, deep fry 2 wrapped eggs at a time for 2 minutes.

101
Crab Pupus

Ingredients:

> 1 (6-ounce) can Crab meat
> 1 (3-ounce) package Cream cheese or 1/2 cup crumbled tofu, drained
> 1/2 teaspoon Soy sauce
> 1/8 teaspoon Garlic powder
> Several drops Tabasco
> 1 pound Won Ton skins
> 1 Egg yolk, beaten

Shred crab meat, removing cartilage. Blend crab with cream cheese, soy sauce, garlic, and Tabasco. Put about 1/2 teaspoon of crab into the center of each Won Ton skin. Moisten edges with egg. Pick up the four corners and pinch them together.

In deep fryer, deep fry 3 or 4 at a time, turning once, until desired brownness is reached (about 2 minutes). Remove from oil and drain on absorbent paper. Repeat until all Pupus are cooked. May be served with cocktail sauce

102
Seafood Pinwheels

Ingredients:
>6 cooked frozen or canned Crab or shrimp
>1 tablespoon Lemon juice
>1 (8-ounce) package Cream cheese
>1/4 teaspoon Celery or garlic salt
>1/8 teaspoon White pepper
>1/4 cup Finely chopped water chestnuts
>1/4 cup Finely chopped green onions
>60 Won Ton wrappers (1-pound)
>1 Egg white, lightly beaten OR 1 tablespoon flour
>mixed with 2 tablespoons cold water

Rinse and drain seafood thoroughly. Shred crab or chop shrimp to make about 1 cup; sprinkle lemon juice over seafood. Beat cream cheese and seasonings until smooth and creamy. Stir in seafood, chestnuts, and onions. Makes 2 cups

Place a scant teaspoon of seafood mixture in center of each won ton wrapper. Brush edges of wrapper with lightly beaten egg white or 1 tablespoon flour mixed with 2 tablespoons cold water. Bring the 4 corners up over filling and pinch together. Pinch edges together and shape to resemble a pinwheel. Keep covered as you work. In deep fryer, deep fry 3 or 4 pinwheels at a time for 2 to 3 minutes. Makes about 60

103
Pumpkin Doughnuts with Spiced Brown Butter Glaze

Ingredients:
    3 1/2 cups All-purpose flour, divided
    1 cup Sugar
    3 teaspoons Baking powder
    1 teaspoon Salt
    1 teaspoon Ground cinnamon
    1 teaspoon Ground ginger
    1/4 teaspoon Ground cloves
    3/4 cup Canned solid pack pumpkin
    4 tablespoons unsalted butter, melted
    2 Eggs plus 1 egg yolk

Sift 1 cup flour, sugar, baking powder, salt, and spices into mixing bowl. In separate bowl, stir together pumpkin, butter, and eggs. Add to dry ingredients and mix on medium speed until smooth, about 30 seconds. Add remaining 2 1/2 cups flour and mix on low speed until just combined, about 30 seconds.

Turn out onto floured surface and let sit 15 minutes. Roll out to 1/2-inch thickness with floured rolling pin, or pat out with floured hands. Cut out doughnuts and holes with floured cutter. Transfer to a baking sheet lined with wax paper. Brush off excess flour. Let sit 15 minutes.

Meanwhile preheat oil in deep fryer. Fry 1 to 2 doughnuts at a time until golden, about 1 minute per side. Drain on paper towels. Dip warm doughnuts in glaze. Transfer to rack or tray until set.

-Spiced Brown Butter Glaze-

3 tablespoons Unsalted butter
1 cup Confectioners' sugar
1/2 teaspoon Ground cinnamon
1/2 teaspoon Ground ginger
Pinch Salt
1/2 teaspoon Vanilla
1 or 2 tablespoons Milk
1 cup Walnuts, lightly toasted, and chopped

Melt butter in small saucepan over low heat. When melted, continue to heat butter over moderate heat until it begins to brown. Watch carefully. Remove from heat as soon as butter reaches a golden brown color. It will move quickly from golden to black (burnt) if not watched. Let cool.

In small bowl, sift together sugar and spices. Gradually mix in cooled butter, vanilla, and enough milk for desired consistency. Sprinkle chopped walnuts over glazed doughnuts.